CAR DRIVING IN TWO WEEKS

and

HINTS FOR ALL MOTORISTS

(Includes Highway Code)

PART 1   LEARNER

PART 2   ADVANCED

"If you carry out the instructions in this book you should become one of the finest drivers in the world."

Includes

THE HIGHWAY CODE

A SERIOUS MATTER

At the time of writing, accidents in Britain have increased about 20% in 12 months. One person per 1,000 Vehicles is killed on our narrow roads, and about 300,000 injured. During your life you have one chance in three of being injured if you are only an *average* driver.

DO NOT BE PENNY WISE AND BUY AN INEXPENSIVE SHORT BOOK WHICH WE BELIEVE CAN-NOT PROVIDE THE INSTRUCTION REQUIRED

OUR GUARANTEE

CAR DRIVING IN TWO WEEKS

AND

HINTS FOR ALL MOTORISTS
AND OTHER ROAD USERS

BY

LAWRENCE NATHAN

Formerly Branch Manager with the British School of Motoring, Ltd.
Founder of the Rightway Schools of Motoring
Recipient of the Certificate of the Royal Society
for the Prevention of Accidents
Registered Driving Instructor
with the R.A.C. Diploma

PART 1 LEARNER
PART 2 ADVANCED

Includes The Highway Code

ELLIOT RIGHT WAY BOOKS,
KINGSWOOD, SURREY, U.K.

17th EDITION   1st IMPRESSION

Accepted by experts as the
standard work on the subject.

Used by many motor schools
as their text book.

The Highway Code is included by kind permission of The Controller H.M.
Stationery Office.

Made and Printed in Great Britain by C. Nicholls & Company Ltd.
Manchester

Contents

CONTENTS

PART TWO

Advice to the more Advanced Driver

Diagrams

THE HIGHWAY CODE

NOTICE TO NEWSPAPERS
AND MAGAZINES

In the interest of road safety, the publishers are pleased to grant free permission to newspapers and magazines to quote an extract of up to 250 words, provided acknowledgement is given in the following terms:—

From "Car Driving in Two Weeks"
Published by Elliot Right Way Books
Kingswood, Surrey
(Bound 7/6d., Paper-back edition 3/6d.)

Foreword

THE title "Car Driving in Two Weeks" does not mean that everyone of seventeen or over can pass the test in so short a time – although they should be able to do so. Some may take longer but that does not mean they will not succeed. The author has been personally responsible for thousands of motorists passing the modern Driving Test.

You will read of the faults and remedies which are looked for by Test Examiners. If the instruction in this book is put into practice, always assuming there is a commonsense attitude, associated with good road-sense, and remembering never to insist on your "right-of-way" whilst driving, you should pass the Test. But there is no "easy" road.

Ninety per cent of Test failures are due to inexperience in traffic. But to have had a lot of experience is not sufficient to gain a pass, if that experience includes mistakes made which show an Examiner that a candidate had not got a "clue" as to the requirements. If you digest the following pages, you should not only find the "clue", but solve the enigma : How to "Pass" the Driving Test.

It is, of course, assumed you can start, stop, and change the gears; also that you can steer the car in a straight line, in forward and in reverse gear.

As you proceed to assimilate carefully the contents of this book, many things will be brought to your notice – things you should or should not do in your method of stopping, starting, gear-changing, and a hundred-and-one little mistakes which, added together, result in a Test failure.

Many have been taught to drive by a friend but, because the teacher has never had to pass a modern Driving Test, he cannot give the type of instruction which the Ministry of Transport Driving Examiners expect. *Today, the "L" driver must be good to pass.*

Unless the learner has had expert tuition there is the danger of his unconsciously acquiring bad driving habits. Thousands of so-called drivers with many miles to their credit have developed incorrect habits which are passed on unintentionally to any beginner they may be teaching. These faults would cause a candidate to fail.

During your Test run remember the following "Driving Philosophy":

1. There is an invisible car behind you and the invisible driver is watching for your signals.
2. The vehicle immediately in front of you has a printed poster tacked to its rear.
   On it are the words: "I am going to stop – can you?"
3. Everyone on the road, including pedestrians, is mentally deficient, therefore it all depends on you.

Remember, on Test is the first time that you are in absolute charge of the car. You are on your own. You cannot expect nor will you get any help whatsoever from the examiner. He is there to see if you are safe, courteous and competent to drive. If it becomes necessary for the examiner to pull on the hand-brake or to assist with the steering in order to avoid a collision, then you MUST FAIL.

THE AUTHOR WARNS YOU

A Personal Message

THIS book is written with the conviction that there is no magic way to overcome the difficulties of learning to pass the Test.

This does not mean there are insurmountable difficulties nor that the road to success is too severe; provided you realize the necessity to convince a Ministry of Transport Examiner that you are competent to drive safely, and put into practical application, during the Test run, your knowledge of the Highway Code.

In thirty years experience I have driven an automobile millions of miles, on most of our minor roads and all of our major roads in all kinds of weather. Although I hold a driving licence which has no blemish I make no claim this is unique. But I do assert that to have done so is not due to luck. There are great differences between the good "steerer" and the good "driver". I will point these out and indicate the many pitfalls you can meet during your Test.

All your motoring life, and particularly on your Test run, if the element of doubt what to do once flits across your mind then – DON'T do it.

If under any circumstances there is *no element of doubt* whatever, then get it done. *Do not linger once you have decided.*

Example: You are about to overtake – you look in your driving mirror, you signal your intention, but as you are about to do so you realize there is an oncoming vehicle. You dither – shall you overtake or not? You see what I mean? Here is the element of doubt.

If you dither on Test it is fatal. The Examiner concludes your "dither" is due to lack of experience so he fails you.

The Ministry of Transport Driving Test is standardized throughout the country. But remember that although the Test requirements are standardized, you cannot standardize the decision of the individual Examiner. There will always be the human element.

11

Your standard of general driving ability, plus a correct interpretation of the exact requirements as laid down by the Ministry of Transport (these requirements you will find on the back of the form, "Application for the Driving Test"), and your performance as seen through the eyes of the Driving Examiner, will determine your success – or otherwise. The Test takes approximately thirty to forty minutes or sometimes one hour. There are certain things you should and should not do.

The Examiner will ask you various questions on the Highway Code and the Rules of the Road.

Many will ask you questions about other aspects of motoring, all of which are thoroughly covered and explained later.

A check will be taken on your eyesight. You will be asked to read a number-plate on a stationary vehicle some twenty-five yards distant.

Do not think that the Test is easy; it is not. You have got to be good. A lot of people have wrong ideas about it. One hears of the person who was "trapped" whilst on Test; of others who failed "through no fault of their own".

In a wide experience of Test conditions and requirements, I am convinced that Ministry of Transport Tests are conducted in a most fair manner. There are no "traps". Everything is honest. Some Examiners are more exacting than others, and require a higher standard but you may be sure that if on Test you give a safe exhibition, and have a working knowledge of the Highway Code, then the most exacting of Examiners will give you a certificate.

I have sometimes heard it said that "So-and-so" passed the Driving Test by offering a bribe. This I do not believe. Many do fail and because of a psychological reason – a dislike of admitting that they were incompetent, or just "not ready" to take the Test – will invent a plausible excuse.

I quote two or three of the many excuses offered. "The Examiner asked me the time, I took my hand off the wheel to look at my wrist watch, and because I did so he failed me"; or, "The Examiner asked me to 'step-on-it', and because I did so he failed me." Then there was the person who was asked by the Examiner to drive into a no-entry street and because this

person refused to do so was "failed". To this there is one reply –
Nonsense !

On your Driving Test, you are either ready and fit to pass or
you are not. *You cannot fool the driving examiner.*

If you pass you will be asked to sign a pink-coloured certificate which you will then be given. This pink slip exempts you
from the necessity of an L plate or an accompanying driver. You
do not need to apply for a full licence until the provisional one
expires. Keep the pink pass and on expiry date of licence take
both to Licensing Authority when you will get full licence
which lasts three years and costs 15/-.

Should you fail the Examiner will tender his regrets, then
hand to you a buff-coloured slip. Upon this will be crosses, put
there in ink by the Examiner; the crosses will be opposite the
different items with which you have not complied. The Examiner may say to you, "Apply for another Test in a month".
This is the minimum before you can again take the Test.

Should this happen, do not despair; there are instances of
people failing to pass the Test except after many attempts.
About forty-three per cent get through the first time and of
those who study this book carefully the figure is probably double
that or more. Study the Highway and Motorway Code as carefully.

The 39 Faults

The police give thirty-nine faults as contributing to the 65,210 accidents in which car drivers were involved. *Think about them.* In order of seriousness they included:

FAULT.	ACCIDENTS
Crossing without due care at road junction	11,174
Turning right without due care	8,691
Excessive speed having regard to conditions	5,307
Misjudging clearance, distance or speed	4,778
Overtaking improperly on off side	4,385
Inattentive or attention diverted	3,675
Driver negligently opening side door	2,682
Stopping suddenly	2,549
Failing to comply with traffic sign or signal	2,419
Failing to keep to near side of proper traffic lane	2,403
Losing control	2,358
Swerving	1,740
Following another vehicle too closely	1,606
Turning left without due care	1,548
Failing to stop at pedestrian crossings	1,223
Learner driver	1,183
Pulling out from near side without due care	902
Dazzled by lights of another vehicle	891
Reversing negligently	877
Other error of judgement or negligence	863
Under the influence of drink or drug	642

Other factors in accidents included: Negligently turning round in road (519), cutting in (449), inexperience with type of vehicle in use at the time (372), fatigue or sleep (278), moving off without taking proper precautions (263), illness (230), changing traffic lane without due care (180) and being hampered by a passenger, an animal or luggage inside the car (49).

The above "39 Faults" are taken from The Daily Telegraph by their kind permission.

CHAPTER ONE

For the Absolute Beginner

THE beginner finds difficulty in knowing when to change a gear. A start will be made in first (or low) gear and, providing there has not been a "buck jumping" performance, second gear will probably be engaged after a few minutes. The "buck jumping" is because the clutch pedal has been released hastily. *Remember that it is the last half inch of clutch release that counts.*

Where possible the novice should practise brakes and clutch, on an open piece of ground, or his own drive, before going out on busy roads.

Many learners assume that "slow clutch-pedal release" is correct. Actually this is not so, and is seen to be incorrect, because a slow release of the clutch-pedal usually results in loss of speed. The word SLOW should be changed to SMOOTH. It would be wiser if the learner regarded the use of clutch-pedal and gear-change thus: When changing gear, "make haste *smoothly."*

With a view to enlightening the absolute beginner as to the purpose of the clutch, without being technical, it should be understood that on a modern car it is possible (and happens with learners!) to change gear without using the clutch at all. In other words, the gears can be crashed or slammed in without first squeezing down the clutch-pedal. It can be done, but it is obviously incorrect.

The purpose of the clutch is to ease the application of the load from one gear to another, and to assist you to make an easy change whilst travelling at speed. Incidentally, the "load" referred to in the previous sentence is the "weight" of the car.

Most learners have difficulty when starting from stop. As long as the car is in motion and it is a case of steering along a straight road, everything goes smoothly.

If using choke to start remember to close it after a few seconds or minutes, otherwise the car tends to "run-away" –

especially noticeable if stopping. If this happens "both feet down" and into neutral.

Trouble begins when the learner has to stop for an emergency. At the moment of moving away all sorts of little things arise to upset him. He will be at the line where he has stopped, say, at the traffic lights and as he is moving off a belated vehicle will come into the line of vision, or a careless pedestrian saunters across the road; and all goes wrong.

The hand-brake is *not* released, the clutch is released, the car gives a violent shudder and stops. Then the beginner gets panicky. The gear is in first, the starter is switched on, pulled (or pushed), the clutch pedal has not been depressed and wow! the car jerks forward.

Worst of all when this happens on a hill. As the hand-brake if released too soon will cause the car to slip backwards, a wild grab is made for the hand-brake, but in the excitement the foot is taken off the clutch-pedal and again the engine stalls. So it goes on. Try to be cool, calm and collected, and you can if you study clutch control in Chapters Six and Eight.

Learner-drivers usually loiter too long in the lower gears, or change up to third and fourth too soon. It is wiser to *allow the speedometer to determine when gears should be changed* until you are able to judge. See Chapter Two. A quick glance at the speedometer is all you need; then *eyes back to the road*.

On entering any car
check these VITAL points:

(a) That gear lever is in neutral – otherwise on starting car may jerk forward and kill someone. See that hand-brake is on before starting up.

(b) That all doors are properly closed.

(c) That driver's seat is firmly fixed (and suitably adjusted).

(d) Driving mirrors are adjusted for *you*.

CHAPTER TWO

Gear Changes in Relation to Speed

TIME comes when by practice the novice begins to understand the language of the engine. A car engine speaks a language all its own. The experienced driver has learned to understand this language, and by virtue of this acquired knowledge, can change the gears by sound.

The sooner the novice begins to understand this language, the more rapid his progress. Here is a foolproof formula which will enable the novice to change the gears at the correct time always. It will be found easy to learn and can be applied with confidence.

By using the formula, the day will come when, by application of this method, plus an association of ideas, gears will be changed and the novice will suddenly realize that the gears have been changed without using the formula. The novice is no longer a novice, the language of the engine is being subconsciously understood; gear changing has become automatic and easy. The formula can be used with any car or motor vehicle and a slight variation will not affect the ultimate result. (Excepting Chapter Sixteen and Seventeen).

"FORMULA FOR GEAR CHANGES IN RELATION TO SPEED" FOR THE "FOUR FORWARD SPEED" GEAR BOX

Up to : 5 m.p.h. and not exceeding   1st (or low) gear
Up to : 8 m.p.h. and not exceeding 10 m.p.h.   2nd gear
Up to : 15 m.p.h. and not exceeding 20 m.p.h.   3rd gear
At   21 m.p.h. and over   4th gear (top)

FOR THE "THREE FORWARD SPEED" GEAR BOX

Up to : 5 m.p.h. and not exceeding   1st gear
Up to : 10 m.p.h. and not exceeding 15 m.p.h.   2nd gear
From   15 m.p.h. to 18–20 m.p.h. engage 3rd gear (top)

With modern high-powered cars the speeds could be increased as follows:

Up to: 10 m.p.h.	1st gear
5 m.p.h. up to 40 m.p.h.	2nd gear
15 m.p.h. up to 65 m.p.h.	3rd gear
Over 20 m.p.h.	4th gear

But this is hardly a beginner's type of car.

Note: When climbing, increase the mileage per hour by five. When going downhill the miles per hour can be *reduced* two or three. (See Chapter Fifteen).

Do not be confused with these tables in their relationship to gears and speed ratios, as compared to the methods of using the engine (by medium of the gears) for *braking* purposes or ordinary *climbing* purposes. Nothing alters the formula for gear-change usage *when starting from stop on a level road*. YOU MUST, OF COURSE, LEARN TO CHANGE GEARS WITHOUT TAKING YOUR EYES OFF THE ROAD.

APPROACH SPEED at *all* cross-roads and junctions should be a *maximum* of 10 m.p.h. using 2nd gear. As road-end nears, reduce speed to 3 to 5 m.p.h. using foot-brake and *cover* the clutch-pedal. Do *not* allow foot to *rest* on clutch, unless using it. Look Right, Left, and Right again before emerging. If safe ... proceed. If you have to stop for safety then engage hand-brake and *1st gear*.

HALT SIGNS:—Approach in 3rd gear (2nd gear if 3-speed gear-box), at a maximum speed of 10 m.p.h. STOP with nose of vehicle *on Halt* line. Engage hand-brake then 1st gear. Look Right, Left, and Right again – proceed *only* if safe to do so.
TRAFFIC LIGHTS:—Approach in 3rd gear (2nd gear if 3-speed gear-box) unless you have seen the change to green within the last 30 yards of approach. Maximum speed of approach about 15 m.p.h. *Never* attempt to beat the lights. If you have to stop at a Red traffic light engage hand-brake and put gear-lever into *neutral* whilst waiting, and take your foot OFF the clutch. Dip clutch-pedal on Amber and engage 1st gear, moving off on Green. If the lights are on a hill you will need to use the hand-

brake to hold the car while stopped. Always release hand-brake when you move off.

SECOND MIRROR:—It is a good idea for your instructor to fit an extra inside mirror. The suction "stick-on" type are inexpensive at chain stores.

On Test it is now a must to engage hand-brake if stopped at halt-signs, slow-signs, cross-roads, traffic-lights and while waiting to turn right in centre of road.

CHAPTER THREE

The "Smooth" Take-Off

ASSUMING your car engine is functioning correctly, you will find that to prevent stalling of engine the following procedure is infallible:

Each time you start *check* your gear lever and see that it is in the *Neutral* position. If the engine is not running, you then switch on engine and start it, depress clutch-pedal and engage low (first gear). Your engine is now slowly ticking over. Before allowing the clutch-pedal to come up give *gentle* acceleration . . . no jerks.

If car is on a level road release hand-brake so that you can start. The purr of the engine should now be more distinct. You have accelerated the "beat" of the engine from a "tick" to a "revolution". Maintain the louder engine "rev" by keeping accelerator-pedal gently squeezed down, but *not* too much.

It is incorrect to lift the foot on and off the accelerator-pedal. Squeeze gently down *once* and when you get the increased "beat" maintain it. Keep the pedal still. Then allow the clutch-pedal to come up *smoothly*.

It should be understood that it is the LAST HALF-INCH OF CLUTCH-PEDAL RELEASE THAT COUNTS. The last half-inch before the clutch-plates are completely engaged is the vital moment. It is perfect control of this last half-inch which determines a nice smooth get-away or a violent one.

Hold the pressure on the *last* half-inch of clutch until the car is moving away. When the car is on the move *smoothly*, *let-up* this last half-inch. There will be no jerk. At this time the accelerator should still be held in the same position. As the car is moving away and the *clutch*-pedal is being released, you apply a gentle, firmer squeeze on the *accelerator* so that the car picks up greater speed.

There is a wrong impression that it is the *petrol* which determines the get-away of a car. It is not. *The control of clutch is the deciding factor.*

At the moment a gear is being changed the accelerator should be completely released. You should not supply petrol to the engine *until* the gear is engaged and the clutch-pedal is *almost* completely released. This sequence should be carried out in each gear-change from low to top. Practise it.

Some reader who has technical knowledge may disagree with this method. I am not interested; my purpose is to enable readers to pass the Driving Test.

Imagine the sole of your shoe as being *glued* to the surface of the clutch-pedal. You squeeze down together and in the same way the clutch-pedal should *come up* as if it were "glued" to your shoe. Do not allow the sole of the shoe to leave it until the pedal has completely returned to the original position (as when not being used).

Imagine what would happen if you depressed a powerful spring with your foot and then suddenly lifted it away. The spring would "jump" back. This happens if the foot is jerked too quickly off the clutch. Motto: A SMOOTH, EVEN, CONTINUOUS RELEASE. "Hold" clutch-pedal until vehicle moves and then ease the foot slowly and smoothly away.

This holding of clutch-pedal should not be over-done. Practice will show the correct time to "hold" and how and when to release.

A gear is first *selected* but is not *engaged* until the clutch-pedal is released. As the clutch-pedal is released the gear previously selected becomes *operative* and the car moves away in the gear selected, assuming that gentle acceleration is given upon the last half-inch of clutch-pedal release.

CHAPTER FOUR

Method to Adopt for Using Gear Lever

THE ball on the top of the gear-lever should not be "clawed". Do not bend the fingers round the top of the ball, except when reverse gear is such that the lever has to be *lifted*. Allow the ball to fit into the palm of the hand, then lead the gear in the direction wanted, palm of the hand facing the way to go.

Visualize a capital letter H with the gear-lever in the centre line of the H. This gear-lever comes up from the centre line of the H and enables you to select a gear as you move about within the various lines which form the H. (Imagine the lines of the H are "lanes or channels" for the purpose of this illustration). Different makes of cars can have the position of the gears in different corners of the H. Get a mental picture of the various gear positions in the vehicle you are driving, and, when changing from a gear to another, face the palm of your hand the way you want lever to go. Lead the gear-lever towards the gear you desire (having first depressed the clutch-pedal) and with a confident *easy ... through ...* movement, select the new gear.

When changing from one gear to another you are leading the "gear-lever" along the lanes/channels which form the imaginary H. Each selected gear is at the *end* of each corner of the H. To clear up a point there is no such thing as a ... "Neutral Gear". When the lever is in the "Neutral-Lane" the gears are disengaged. Immediately you have selected the new gear allow the clutch-pedal to come up ... *smoothly*, and accelerate away.

CHAPTER FIVE

Steering Column Gear Control

(WORKS BY REMOTE CONTROL)

PEOPLE who have never used the steering-column gear have often asked me how it works. Surprisingly, it operates (so far as the user is concerned) in the same way as the ordinary gear-lever.

Regard the steering-column gear-lever as "remote" control; it is "remote" in relation to the gears which are to be operated. The ordinary type of lever is closer to the gear-box.

The synchromatic gear-change requires the use of a clutch, as does the "ordinary" type. You depress the clutch-pedal and change gears normally.

Remember, as in different makes of cars with the "joystick" gear-lever, the positions of the gears are not standardized in the steering-column gear-change. Why? Well, that is one of the idiosyncrasies of the manufacturers. You get the old type of gear-change with reverse gear next to number four gear, or next to number one gear, and so on. Similiarly with the new. Irrespective of the position in the gear-box of the gears, the principle and operation (for the user) are the same.

Imagine the old-type gear-box as being shaped like the capital letter H. Ignore meantime, the reverse gear, and assume we are dealing with a gear-box which contains four forward gears. (It is the same with the three forward gear-box). The capital H, for our purpose is now the symbol of the old-type gear-box.

Therefore, to enable you to visualize the steering-column type of gear-change, tip over on to its side this symbol, the capital H. You now get the horizontal line (the long arm of the H) with its neighbour running horizontally with it, above it. In the centre is the short connecting vertical arm. This is the neutral lane (or channel) in the mechanism of our steering-column gear-changing unit.

If you have followed clearly you should now have a mental

picture of the pattern of the new-type gear-changing unit.

Take the mental picture and make it a "remote" unit (i.e. remote from the gear-box which, of course, is under the floor-boards). This "remote" control is brought about by a series of linkups from the gear-box to the steering-column.

The gear-lever which juts out from the steering-column is the medium you use when changing from one gear to the other. To enable you to do this, there is (within the steering-column itself) our old friend the letter H, which, if you recall, is tipped over on to its side but otherwise the same as the floor-board H as dealt with in Chapter 4. When the gear lever is free (no gear engaged) it is in the neutral lane.

To engage first gear (or number one) push the lever towards number one. The palm of the hand is facing the way you want to go. Half-way between one and two is the neutral lane. You now wish to engage second. With the palm of your hand facing downwards pull lever towards you, into number two.

From second to third gear. Face the palm of the hand upwards, then push towards the neutral lane. At the neutral lane lift and then push forward again into number three.

From three into four. Palm of the hand faces upwards and pull towards you, remembering that as you pull towards you from three to four, it is very important to press palm of hand upwards at the same time the whole of the time, until fourth is engaged.

Should you not press *up* from three to four, you may easily "grind" into second gear.

Of paramount importance when changing gears (where a gear-lever is used) is to remember the rule: *Palm of the hand the way you want the lever to go.* Here is a valuable practical hint for practice.

Draw the H on to a postcard, about two inches square. Then cut it out, and place a match through the centre. The match is the gear-lever in Neutral and is plumb centre of the neutral lane.

If you turn on to its side the entire figure you have cut out (leaving the match stuck in its neutral position) you will then have a replica of the synchromatic stéering-column gear-changing apparatus.

CHAPTER SIX

Clutch Control (Starting on a Hill)

THE start-away when on a hill can be a menace to the learner. Here is when perfect clutch control is a boon. Under Test conditions the vehicle must not slip back, at any time, not even one inch.

Strangely enough, there are drivers with years of experience who still allow the vehicle to slip back when starting away on a gradient. There are still many more who get away without slipping, but do so with a terrific petrol waste and a roaring engine. This method is not only unnecessary but shows a lack of clutch control.

Here is a foolproof method which ensures a slow, smooth get-away always, even on the steepest of gradients.

The vehicle is stationary on a hill (going up). The hand-brake is on and the engine is running; the gear lever is in neutral and both feet are off the pedals. You first depress the clutch-pedal, then push the gear-lever into low gear position. Now change the beat of the engine (as previously stated) by gentle acceleration. When you get a steady, strong purr, or a little louder engine revolution, keep it. You must hold the right foot *perfectly still* once the louder engine beat is heard. Then smoothly allow the clutch-pedal to come up; as the clutch-pedal is coming up (the acceleration is still being held in "revolution" position) listen carefully for the tone of the engine to alter. You should hear the tone dying down.

The clutch-plates are now engaging and you have CLUTCH CONTROL. Now is the time to release the hand-brake (making sure that the hand-brake is absolutely released – not half on). But – and this is important – although you now release the hand-brake you still maintain the clutch-pedal in the *exact position* it was in when you heard the tone of the engine die away. *The vehicle will now remain stationary without slipping back, and without the hand-brake on.*

All that remains is to allow the *last half-inch* of clutch to come up fully and smoothly and the vehicle will move smoothly and slowly up the hill. As it commences you apply further, gentle, firmer acceleration. If you practise this method you will gradually be able to do everything quicker and snappier.

"Flogging the engine!" This expression is often not understood by many learners or even many older drivers. Like the callous horse driver who "flogs" his horse with a whip when the beast is pulling a heavy load *uphill*, the car driver "flogs" his engine by too much acceleration, especially uphill. When starting up on a *very* steep hill, i.e. the Hill-Start on Test, after the car is on its way do *not* over-accelerate. If the brow of the hill is some twelve to twenty yards from your starting-away point then stay in first gear until you are over the brow before changing up into second gear. But give just enough petrol to do the job. Do not flog your engine.

CHAPTER SEVEN

Emergency Stop Under Control (On Test)

ON Test you will probably be asked to do an *emergency* stop. If this is the Examiner's intention he should say to you *before* you start the Test, "Sometime, somewhere I will want an Emergency Stop, your indication to *stop* will be when I tap the dashboard or my knee with my hand". (Sometimes the tap will be given by a newspaper, etc., or verbally.)

Immediately you get this signal to *stop* ... *do so* ... as fast as you can. Do not worry about danger from behind ... STOP. (The Examiner has checked behind before you are asked.)

BOTH FEET DOWN

Do not give a stopping slow-down signal ... do not worry about driving-mirror ... get your foot on to foot-brake FAST and follow IMMEDIATELY by getting clutch-pedal down also ... to prevent stalling of engine. BOTH FEET DOWN. Keep both hands on steering-wheel and keep straight course. Should the signal to stop be given as you are about to change gear ... ignore the gear change and STOP. Some Examiners give this Emergency Stop as you have just got round a left-hand turn ... *wherever* you are ... STOP.

When the car is at a standstill put on the *hand-brake* ... bring the gear-lever into NEUTRAL position ... but *do not* switch off the engine unless the Examiner asks.

IMPORTANT WARNING

Occasionally a test or practice is done in rain or icy conditions so we refer to a stop in emergency UNDER CONTROL.

Obviously the braking instructions given above MUST BE INTERPRETED IN RELATION TO THE ROAD SURFACE CONDITIONS. The best braking result is that achieved without actually locking the wheels. The wording *Both Feet Down fast* applies but do *not* stamp *fiercely* on the brakes in bad weather.

This could involve you in a dangerous or serious skid, or, at least, a Test failure.

NEED FOR PRACTICE

In emergencies (except skidding) e.g. if accelerator-pedal sticks "ON", you normally think and act "*both feet hard down*".

The primary purpose of the Test Emergency Stop is to check reaction, how fast can you transmit from brain to feet. It is something *all* learners should *practise a lot* before they go on to the road. *Both feet down* is the *life-saving technique*.

If you wish to save on brake-linings and tyres, practise while stationary. The reason for the need of practice is to get yourself used to the feet-down reaction, just for that unexpected emergency. Once this is instinctive you are safer. If practising on the road be sure there is nothing following and that the road is clear and safe, and do not, as a learner, practise on a wet or icy road, owing to the danger of skidding – except with great care and an EXPERIENCED instructor beside you. You must learn complete control in emergency without skidding.

Remember almost every accident is unexpected. Over-confidence is one of the chief causes of fatal accidents. *Insurance statistics prove this.*

A MASTER TIP

On "fast" roads one often sees an accident or "problem" far ahead. Even if you may not have to slow down,
TOUCH YOUR BRAKES SO AS TO
FLICK ON YOUR BRAKE-LIGHTS
This warns those following of possible danger.

IN HEAVY FOG OR SNOW, IF YOU HAVE TO STOP, KEEP BRAKE-LIGHTS ON. (BETTER STILL GET OFF THE ROAD TO AVOID BEING IN A PILE-UP.)

CHAPTER EIGHT

The Learner's Secret

NEXT in importance, perhaps only to the Emergency Stop, is to practise complete Clutch Control. Nearly everything in life is easy, if you know how to do it and driving is no exception. However, not all instructors begin by adequately illustrating the ability to use the clutch, so get your teacher to show you how to hit your target (below). Once you master that you are, to a great extent, master of your job.

YOUR TARGET

To take all of 10 to 15 seconds to move a car over the short distance of 10 yards *without stopping* during the exercise. In other words, to gain the control of the clutch required, to be able to cause the car to move at the speed of a fast snail.

Use an open space or quiet road to practise this art of controlling the clutch and *keep practising* it until you can do it both in forward and reverse gear. From that point forward many other matters will become easier.

THE METHOD

In controlling "snail" speed you "slip the clutch", i.e. you do NOT allow it to come up entirely but maintain it at the position *required* to keep the snail's pace – at the same time you accelerate only enough to hold the slow speed. Control is achieved by almost imperceptible up and down clutch movement (and steady acceleration). Most drivers rest their heel on the floor, using the heel as a pivot, to control the clutch-pedal (as is done with the accelerator). Practise uphill as well as on the level.

CHAPTER NINE

Expert Method of Starting and Parking on a Hill

THE underlying principle is identical with that in Chapter 6. The difference is in the method adopted to achieve the same result. Everything is done in the same way : the clutch-pedal is depressed, the gear-lever is moved into *low-gear*, the accelerator is "pepped up" slightly, and the clutch-pedal is then allowed to come up *smoothly*.

Instead of listening for a change in the engine tone (difficult under traffic conditions), you will *feel* the vehicle "rarin' to go" (that is when the engine tone alters as it were), yet it cannot get away *because* the hand-brake is on. This is the moment to release the brake, "hold" the clutch-pedal, and, as the vehicle moves, let up *the last bit of clutch-pedal* and apply further gentle acceleration. For reversing uphill, identical methods are used, except that you are, of course, in reverse.

PARKING ON A HILL

On test you will be asked, "What precautions would you take to secure vehicle if leaving it unattended on a hill?" The answer is you would leave vehicle with front wheels turned into kerb, hand-brake at ON position and in *reverse* gear ... if facing downhill. For uphill, as above but leave in *first* gear. (Personally, when facing up a *steep* hill I run *rear* wheels into kerb and leave in *first* gear with hand-brake on). *Lock doors* to prevent entry by thieves, or children who may cause car to "run away".

On TEST ... MOVING at a VERY SLOW WALKING speed ... UPHILL

You may be asked to take a left or right-hand turn into a street which rises *very steeply* and as you are climbing and have gone up the gear-box to 2nd or 3rd gear, the Examiner may say

"I want you to continue driving up this hill at a *slow walking speed*" ... that is as slow as a fast snail.

You change-down *immediately* from 3rd to 2nd and from 2nd to 1st. It is *fatal* to stall the engine or to run back downhill.

Immediately you have *selected* the lower gear (to do so you must almost stop, slow down to about 3 m.p.h.) allow the clutch-pedal to come up smartly ... but not ... fast or with a jerk, and *increase* the acceleration. When you are using the 1st gear allow the clutch-pedal to come up ... but ... use as in the hill start (see previous), but do not actually stop.

This should be practised during your lessons.

STARTING DOWNHILL

Engage 1st gear (if a steep hill 2nd gear) put foot on *foot-brake*, release hand-brake, and allow car to go forward by gently releasing foot-brake. As you do so, release clutch smoothly and apply acceleration as required, changing to higher gear as needed.

CHAPTER TEN

Worries of the "L" Driver whilst on Test

WORRIES begin immediately something unexpected happens, because you are not "ready" for the Test. Be sure you have had sufficient experience in traffic before you apply.

Assuming you feel competent, remember you are still a learner; it is good to have confidence, yet, strangely, many fail because they have too much. They allow this to become enthusiasm, and drive recklessly. It is as great a fault on Test to be over-cautious. To clear up in the minds of learners some of the items which arise on Test to confuse them, they should study the following paragraphs:—

1. You must definitely stop at the Halt sign; to be moving, however slowly, is fatal.
2. Should you be the second or third vehicle in a stream of traffic (or even if you are sixth) and the first stops at the Halt, *you too must stop* when you reach the Halt line. If you are fourth in the queue, and number one halts, then number two and number three follow on without stopping, *you* must not fall into this trap. The two in front who did not stop were wrong; but *they* are *not* on Test.
3. The same applies should you encounter pedestrians on an uncontrolled pedestrian crossing. Suppose you are following another vehicle, there are pedestrians on the crossing, the driver in front sounds his horn, holds up the people on the crossing and proceeds. If you follow the example, you will fail. Under no circumstances should you sound the horn when approaching an uncontrolled crossing if people are on it. It should be understood that a pedestrian has 'ALWAYS the right-of-way.

There has been a lot of controversy about the right-of-way of a pedestrian. The majority of learners, and unfortunately a great number of so-called experienced drivers have an incorrect view.

When they are asked, "When has a pedestrian the right-of-way?" nine out of ten reply, "When on a Zebra crossing," and "If the traffic light is for them," (i.e., If the light is at red against the motorist, then the green light is for the pedestrian). Alternatively, some will include the pedestrian as having the right-of-way if a policeman is on control at a crossing. The assumption is that apart from the instances quoted, the pedestrian never has the right-of-way. How wrong this is.

Had we a better understanding there would be fewer accidents. If you gave the matter thought it would be seen that there is only one answer, and if the correct reply be given and understood, then there would be no problem. The answer is summed up in one word – "*always*".

I can visualize the consternation of any reader if he is already a driver and has no Test to pass. "Absurd," – but wait, here is proof. Such readers will, by their own admission, be compelled to accept the veracity of the answer given – "always".

Assume you are driving along a road; assume it is an ordinary road, without Zebra crossings, lights or police control. You are in a built-up area and travelling at 30 miles per hour, and there are vehicles parked on the near-side. About forty feet in front of your vehicle a careless pedestrian steps from between the parked vehicles. He does not know about braking and thinking time in relation to stopping distances. You think fast, you cannot cut into the near-side because of the parked vehicles, you cannot swerve out to the off-side because of oncoming traffic.

So what do you do? Unless you wish to find yourself in Court, you brake with a view to stopping. Yes? No? I rather imagine Yes! But why? The pedestrian is not on a crossing. He is walking unconcernedly across a place where he has no right-of-way. Or has he? He most certainly has. You have given him the right-of-way by virtue of the fact that you have stopped.

In the same way, where a policeman is on traffic control, he waves you through and there are pedestrians on the crossing, *the responsibility is yours* – not the policeman's.

4. You are going towards the traffic lights and the lights change to green! If there are pedestrians on the crossing

(they will now be crossing on a red) you *proceed* with GREAT CARE, stopping if required.

5. You are taking a right- or left-hand turn at the lights (the lights are green for those who travel straight forward): should you turn to the left or right it must be obvious that *you* are now turning *against* the red light, therefore, should pedestrians be on the crossing this time, *you* must *stop* and give them passage.

6. Never attempt to beat the lights.

7. Never attempt to beat anyone to it.

8. Traffic travelling forward has priority over that turning – at any cross-roads (including cross-roads where there is traffic-light control), particularly where a right-hand turn is intended.

9. When you stop for pedestrians on a crossing it should be understood that it is incorrect to wave people through who are actually still on the pavement. If they are on the pavement, even on the causeway edge, you go.

10. If you are taking a left turn and there is a "pedestrian crossing" just on the corner of the street you intend to turn into, but there are no people on it, you anticipate the actions of people who may be going towards the crossing. For example, you intend to turn left, people are walking towards the crossing which you will shortly be travelling over, they have not seen you, they have not seen the signal you have given with the right arm out of the off-side open window (on Test you are allowed to use the indicators, but in addition to the hand signals which must be given, unless the examiner has told you to use "indicators only"); the people who shortly will be on the crossing (on your left – or nearside) must be warned. You do so by a gentle warning on the hooter – gently, not aggressively – you lightly tap the horn. By this indication people will wait on the pavement and allow you to take your turn comfortably.

11. There are times on Test when you find yourself following a slow or horse-drawn vehicle, and you do not know what to do. Overtake, if it is safe to do so. Never loiter behind longer than is necessary. Give horses a wider berth.

HALT! MAJOR ROAD AHEAD

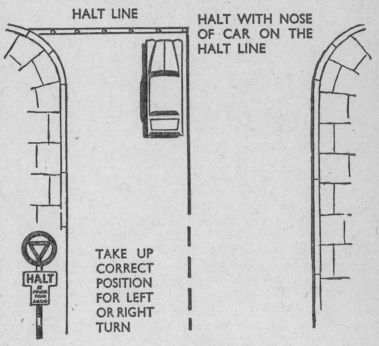

HALT LINE

HALT WITH NOSE
OF CAR ON THE
HALT LINE

HALT
AT
MAJOR
ROAD
AHEAD

TAKE UP
CORRECT
POSITION
FOR LEFT
OR RIGHT
TURN

DIAGRAM 1

12. When stopping – at lights etc., do not make a wild grab for hand-brake. Approaching stop line apply *gentle* increased pressure on foot-brake – and to stop – get both *feet down.* After foot-brake step smartly *on clutch to prevent stalling.* Apply hand-brake and into neutral.

There is a tendency by a lot of old-time drivers, who acquired the bad habit from a method which was used years ago, to step on the clutch-pedal *before* they apply the foot-brake. They fear the engine will stall. What is not appreciated is that *immediately the clutch-pedal is pressed down the vehicle is no long under control* and the driver is free-wheeling or coasting, and under Test conditions this method is frowned upon. Therefore he should practise the method of using first the foot-brake and *then* the clutch-pedal.

Irrespective of the gear, a gentle squeeze on the foot-brake will not stall the engine. The more you squeeze the sooner the vehicle will stop, and this firm, gentle squeeze gives a smoother ride than when you stamp on the brake hard. Passengers don't like hitting the windscreen.

To prevent stalling you *rapidly* step on the clutch *at the right moment.* The engine gives warning of its intention to stall either by a slight "cough" or when the gear stick commences to "quiver". Of course, the engine will stall if you allow the clutch to come up from the floorboards, if the brake is at the "on" position (foot- or hand-brake) when the gears are engaged. ON STOPPING GET INTO NEUTRAL.

13. If the compulsory stop be on a hill you pull on the hand-brake. This should be done *after* you have stopped with your feet. You do not remove your hand from the steering-wheel until the vehicle is stationary. Should the stop be on a level road then it is also wiser to use the hand-brake. The hand-brake is primarily for parking purposes or when starting away on a gradient. It should be remembered that when pulling on the hand-brake the ratchet release slip should be used. This makes for a noiseless application and saves wear of the ratchet teeth. Very important.

14. IMPORTANT. When starting away make sure you release the

hand-brake (if used) and apply gentle acceleration before allowing the clutch-pedal up.

15. A grave mistake is to wander; particularly does this apply when a learner is changing gear or giving a hand signal. Wandering is common when a learner is changing gear on a corner. The wisest course is not to change whilst actually turning. Change either before or after the corner. It is preferable to change down before you get to a corner and steer round with both hands on the wheel. When round, be absolutely sure you have the vehicle under control and travelling straight before changing up again.

16. Should you decide to change a gear for any reason, do it. Don't get hold of the gear-lever as if to change, then take your hand back to the steering-wheel and immediately return it to the lever. This indicates indecision. The Examiner sees this.

17. While you are on Test the Examiner is not looking so much for things you are *doing correctly* as noting the things you are *doing incorrectly*.

18. Never place yourself in a position where the actions of other road users cause you to do the wrong thing.

Following are some illustrations:

(a) You are taking a left-hand corner, as you go slowly round, a pedestrian is crossing the road towards your near-side pavement (on your left) from the opposite side of the road *into which you are turning*. He is not on a "crossing", but he is the type of pedestrian who feels he is entitled to cross a street or road how and when he pleases. Due to inexperience you do not stop and allow him free passage but keep going. You find this pedestrian has caused you to take a "wide" left-hand turn to avoid him. If you take "wide" left-hand turns on Test you fail.

(b) The same thing could happen on a right-hand turn and in an endeavour to get round the person to prevent you stopping, you step on the gas and "cut" your right-hand turn. By cutting right-hand corners you fail.

(c) You are approaching a Zebra crossing and someone is

partly across as you get near; he sees you and then stands still. You have slowed down intending to stop, but because the individual on the crossing has stopped, you think, "This person is a decent one, he has stopped to let me go through," and you proceed. The Examiner makes a note of this. It is a mark against you – *not* for you.

The reason why this pedestrian stopped to let you through is because he thought it would be wiser to be safe rather than sorry ! If you indicate by hand signal that you are going to slow down you will achieve a doubly correct result. Giving the slow-down signal indicates to traffic behind your intention, and you notify the pedestrian by this same signal that you intend to give him his right-of-way.

19. You are following a tramcar (there are some in the world still) and are tempted to overtake it on the right (off-side). This is often done by an experienced driver. On Test, it is wisest to overtake on the near-side when a suitable opportunity presents itself, but not if the tramcar has stopped and is loading or unloading passengers, then if safe, overtake on right.

20. Never place yourself in a position where you find that you are in the "centre" and have a vehicle parked on the near-side, with another vehicle coming in the opposite direction and on your immediate off-side with no room for you.

21. You are travelling along a narrow road, there is a stationary vehicle on the near-side, and an oncoming vehicle. It is *your duty* to stop and give way to the vehicle travelling towards you on the off-side.

22. Always give way to a vehicle which is coming up a hill, if you are going down – when there is insufficient space for you to pass each other.

23. Many learners err when starting after a stop as at traffic lights, cross-roads, etc., because they have not taken the precaution to note, when stopping, to see if slight hill-start acceleration is required to get them away without slipping back. This can easily be seen if the foot is lifted from the foot-brake for a second. Should the vehicle slip

back then it is obvious that the hill-start method should be used. (See Chapter 6).

24. Where a policeman is on traffic control and you are turning right, if he does not wave his arm in front of him go *round* him as if he were the imaginary flag-pole. (See page 100).

25. Some drivers are at a loss to understand the instructions when giving signals before moving out etc. ... Some drivers flick the indicator. This can be confusing to traffic behind *especially* if there is a street on the right, near to the place from where you are trying to pull out. If on Test when moving out from the near-side kerb I suggest a *"moving-out"* (right-turn) signal should be given by *hand*. The important thing is to *look over your right* shoulder. Do not move out until you see it is absolutely safe. Watch ESPECIALLY FOR FAST VEHICLES COMING UP BEHIND.

It is important when *moving off* from near-side NOT to pull out to the crown of road. Move straight ahead and keep left if possible.

If pulling to near-side kerb give a "slow-down" signal. ... The *"slow down"* signal is a MUST on Test.

Practice – practice – and more practice is the only way to become efficient; providing your practice is on the correct basic principles as given here.

CHAPTER ELEVEN

"Tips" for the "L" Driver
EXPERIENCED DRIVERS MAY BENEFIT

IF you spend ten minutes at a busy crossing, you will soon realize why the standard of efficiency required for a Test pass is so high. You will notice many bad drivers. You will perceive the driver who "cuts" a corner, and the driver who does not give right-of-way to pedestrians (on a green-light crossing); plus a host of other bad habits. There will also be the few good drivers.

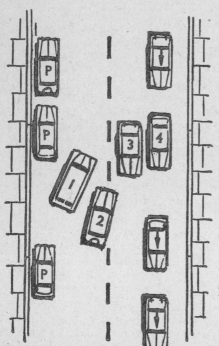

COMMON ACCIDENT

Driver 2 going happily along when driver 1 (often a van) pulls out without checking.

2 swings out to avoid 1 and hits 3. Someone is probably killed.

If 1 had checked this would not have happened.

There are many drivers with years of experience who never give a signal. Some of them actually boast about it and take pride in quoting that "they never bother to signal". So give the no-signal drivers a wide berth.

When you follow such a driver make sure you keep at least three car-lengths behind. Should you be nearer when this type decides to turn or slow-down you may find yourself in a smash.

If you are driving and some yards in front on the near-side is a stationary bus or car, you should *not* take it for granted that the driver of the stationary vehicle is aware that you are coming. As you draw near the stationary vehicle the driver begins to pull away from the kerb and does not signal his intention. You fear running into him and instinctively pull out. The fact that you are now pulling to the off-side, perhaps into oncoming traffic, escapes you. It has happened so quickly you forget to give your hand signal to slow down. So anything can happen. One thinks, "What could be done in such a circumstance?"

A really observant driver, constantly on the alert, who anticipates the possible actions of others, would be prepared for an incident such as this. The driver who is always "on his toes", is ready for any circumstances. He does not panic. Regarding the stationary vehicle which may pull out, as you approach train yourself to glance at the off-side front wheel as you get near. You will then see "wheel movement" if the vehicle moves.

There has been controversy about giving signals. As *seen through the eyes of a Driving Test Examiner and as laid down by a Ministry of Transport instruction, there are no ifs and buts, there is only one correct method.* Give them clearly, concisely, and *in time.*

I find it useful (and often mystifying to any passenger) when, under a condition as follows, I appear to be psychic. You are waiting entry into a Major road, your car is halted and you intend to turn right. There are parked vehicles on the near-side of the road into which you wish to turn; because of this your vision is obstructed and you are undecided as to the safety of proceeding. Some fast vehicle may be coming down the Major road and if so you would be caught in the centre of the intersection as you turned. So you hesitate, you are in a busy part of

KERBSIDE PARKING

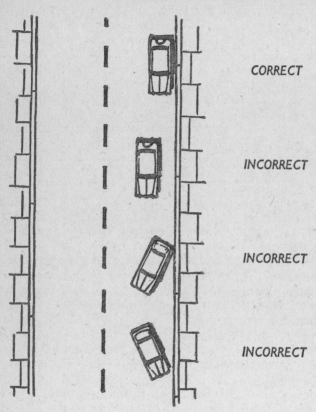

CORRECT

INCORRECT

INCORRECT

INCORRECT

town and the Examiner is sitting patiently beside you. What is there to do?

Frequently under certain conditions, if you look keenly into the shop-windows on the side of the road into which you are about to turn right, you will see the reflection of any vehicle which may be coming, or alternatively the reflection would show if it were safe to proceed. On such "blind" occasions you may need to proceed at a snail's pace till you can see clearly.

Remember if the "L" driver constantly assumed that an invisible vehicle followed him, it would become an instinct to give a signal whenever it became necessary.

The "L" driver should appreciate there are few so-called experienced drivers prepared to show mercy on the road. Suppose the "L" driver is held at a red light, he is the first in a queue, and he is on the brow of a hill. When the time comes to set off the beginner gets excited or is too eager, with the result that he stalls the engine. Then the trouble begins. A selfish driver gets impatient and sounds his horn, this further excites the learner and he "goes to pieces". See what I mean? Don't panic; this is not the end of the world.

The "L" driver should keep his gear in the neutral position when halted for any length of time. Many drivers when halted, immediately get into first or second with the view of a quick get-away. It is a bad practice and should be avoided by beginners.

A tip for all drivers passing a stationary vehicle is to watch carefully underneath for "feet movement" which a pedestrian would make were he to step from behind it. You could see the legs of any person *under* the parked vehicle.

If intending to pass a cyclist, give a *gentle* toot on the horn to advise your approach. As the majority of "L" drivers have difficulty in judging distance when passing other vehicles, *particularly cyclists*, it is wise not to pass too closely. This does not mean a *wide detour* – which could be dangerous.

Learners often find it hard to judge distance when pulling in to the kerb-side when asked to stop. It is usual for them to stop some three feet from the edge. The following enables the beginner to place the vehicle close to the edge. It is essential to keep both hands on the steering wheel, gliding carefully to the stopping place.

On the nose or bonnet of many vehicles is a centrepiece. Sometimes it is a chrome figure, or even just a line or ridge. The point is to get this centrepiece lined up; looking at it from your normal driving position through the windscreen as a means of "lining it up" with the pavement edge. When this "centrepiece" appears to be, say, approximately twelve inches over the pavement your road wheels will be practically six inches away from the edge of the kerb. This does not apply to all cars and you may have to vary the twelve inches.

The ideal travelling position in an ordinary street or busy road is approximately five feet from the near-side kerb. If on a road where there are tram rails, the ideal is to have the tram rail nearest to the near-side kerb dead centre between your two front wheels. Cross tramway rails obliquely, as a cyclist would do. It is folly to ride with your car wheels on the lines, particularly if it is raining, for this can cause skidding. If there is a clear passage (without parked vehicle obstruction) between kerb and tram rails, you should leave the rails and keep left.

SPEED ON TEST

If you are being tested in a restricted area only, *never exceed* 28-30 m.p.h. But, if safe to do so don't loiter at 15 m.p.h. or the Examiner will rightly consider you are under-confident and a nuisance on the road.

If you enter a 40 m.p.h. limit, where safe, step up to 38-40 and if in a de-restricted area proceed at a reasonable speed. Don't drive at high speed, but do not clog up the traffic stream. Keep to the near-side lane moving with the traffic, if you require to overtake, do so with the usual care.

In overtaking, you must be travelling *at least* 5 m.p.h. more than the vehicle you are passing. You then return to the near-side lane – without "Cutting-in" which would be a serious fault.

USE OF MIRROR

On Test (and always) you are expected to look frequently in your mirror so that you ALWAYS know what is following. *It is almost as vital as knowing what is in front.*

CHAPTER TWELVE

Pedestrian Crossings and "Halts"

BEGINNERS are sometimes confused at traffic lights when they have to stop on red. Often there is a row of studs or a line upon which the nose of the car should halt. Sometimes there is no indicating line. In this event the car should stop "this side" of the traffic lights. Where there is a pedestrian crossing at the lights, you should stop "this side" also.

At certain cross-roads, drivers are stopped at a red light whilst *approaching* traffic continues to move. The signal light seen by the oncoming drivers will be *green*. This occurs at some junctions to enable the traffic on the busiest road to proceed for a longer time.

In some areas a road end narrows as you approach the cross-roads. Upon *your* road is *"halt" sign* but the *"halt line"* is further back from the road end than usual. When you halt at this line (as you *must*) it becomes impossible to see traffic which

HALT! MAJOR ROAD AHEAD
(Narrow Road End)

DIAGRAM 2

When Halt line is back from cross-roads, you MUST halt at line. SPECIAL NOTE: At this type of Halt Line ALWAYS stop near your kerb edge even if turning right. This is to leave room for turning traffic.

ZEBRA CROSSING

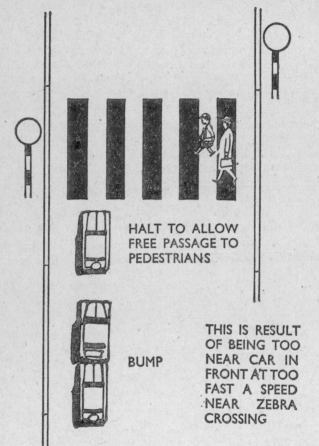

HALT TO ALLOW
FREE PASSAGE TO
PEDESTRIANS

BUMP

THIS IS RESULT
OF BEING TOO
NEAR CAR IN
FRONT AT TOO
FAST A SPEED
NEAR ZEBRA
CROSSING

DIAGRAM 3

may be on the Major road. The reason for the *altered* "halt line" is to enable large vehicles to enter the narrow road without obstruction. *After* your compulsory halt approach the road end very carefully in first or second gear checking to your right, left and right again before turning.

If a policeman is in control at the "Traffic lights" or "Zebra Crossing" change down a gear and reduce speed. Prepare to stop if necessary. If the policeman has held up Pedestrians to enable you to proceed, do so, but with care. Watch for the impulsive pedestrian in a hurry. Accidents happen when least expected . . . in that split second.

Care is needed where an island divides a zebra. You are in order to proceed *if* your portion of the zebra is unoccupied. Except in an emergency never stop *on* a zebra.

BUSES

Bus drivers are apt to think in terms of their "Time Schedule". This can make them careless if running late. The driver has stopped for passengers, he hears the *"go"* bell . . . off he goes. He could have seen you approaching his rear but he has the heavier vehicle and he does not own the bus. From previous experience he EXPECTS (quite wrongly) that you will brake and let him away. What do you do?

As you near a bus glance to see if people are getting on or off, and if they are, glance in your driving mirror and give the "pulling out" signal. Remember, another passenger may be passing the rear or front of the bus intending to cross to your offside. Approach to a stationary bus (in these conditions) means you should probably have changed down and reduced speed, preceded by the slow-down signal. It *may* be necessary to stop.

Be careful of the bus which pulls into the near kerb and then stops *at an angle*, with the near-side rear of the bus into the kerb edge and the *bonnet* about five or six feet away. This means that if it is possible for you to pass this stationary bus *you* must pull

ZEBRA CROSSING NEAR CROSS-ROADS

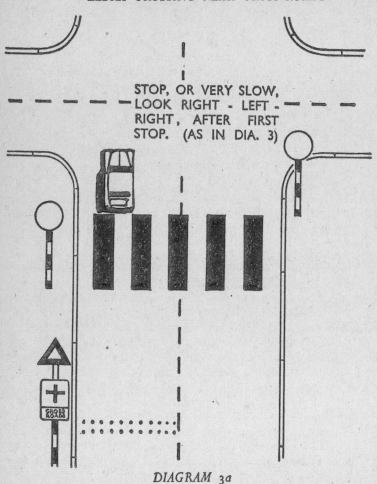

STOP, OR VERY SLOW,
LOOK RIGHT - LEFT -
RIGHT, AFTER FIRST
STOP. (AS IN DIA. 3)

DIAGRAM 3a

A double row of studs in the road 15 yards from the Zebra
Crossing indicates the line beyond which it is illegal to park.

over perhaps to the *other* side of the road. This could be danger-ous . . . take CARE. The moral: IF IN DOUBT . . . DON'T Go. Stop behind the bus but *not too near.* Leave yourself SEEING and getting round distance.

A MASTER TIP

Before crossing any road a driver must always be sure he is accelerating sufficiently, though not roaring the engine, prior to releasing the clutch to enable him to get over *without risk of the engine stalling.* If the engine is cold, unless your car has an automatic choke, you may need to use the choke.

Stalling can also often be due to the hand brake being left "on" or to an incorrect adjustment of the carburet-tor.

Crossing roads or streets is one of the main causes of serious accidents.

"BEWARE TRIANGLES"

Triangles about a foot high, in red, are to be permitted. Placed near the road edge, they will warn approaching traffic of an accident or breakdown. Useful near bends my hope is they might be developed for use in fog to prevent these awful pile-ups.

CHAPTER THIRTEEN

Hand and Indicator Signals

SEE page 175 of the Highway Code. The heading quotes signals by drivers to police constables. There is a signal depicting "I want to Turn *Left*." This picture shows that you cross your arm over your chest. I suggest that instead of doing this you can place your hand flat against the windscreen with the fingers pointing to the left. This signal is accepted as correct.

The majority of learners are woefully lacking in the hand signals part of driving. Some give a correct signal, but give it too soon or too late. Others give two signals when one will do. There are those who stick only their hand out of the window and then "waggle" it about. A slow-down signal appears as if a child were waving good-bye! There is the left-turn signal which often looks like a shake of the hand, as if the driver had palsy. Then you see the lackadaisical right-hand signal, as if it were an effort to put out the hand.

All hand signals should be given in a concise, definite, and distinct motion, in plenty of time, and with as much of your arm out of the window as you can comfortably and safely manage.

An Examiner may ask you only to use hand signals during your Test. Be guided by what he says. The reason for this is that as indicators are a mechanical device, subject to breakdown, you must satisfy the Examiner that you can give the correct hand signals, if and when required.

Note that when the indicator is used *correctly*, by one who is not on Test, it is engaged in plenty of time and remains on usually until a corner has been taken, and is still on when the vehicle is completely round the corner. Mechanical indicators should be cancelled immediately after use if they have not done so automatically.

How annoying it is when you are following a vehicle without this "return to normal" control and for yards in front an indicator remains at a signal position ! This type of carelessness is most confusing to following traffic.

Indicators can be taken as a guide for a hand signal denoting a right or left turn. Visualize yourself as being able to use your indicators whilst on Test and this should enable you to decide *when* to give your hand signal. Be sure it is in plenty of time. Remember, as opposed to the indicator, the hand signal should not be prolonged, and should not continue whilst you are in the act of turning. You must have both hands on the steering-wheel whilst going round.

Do not be confused about giving a signal in time. It is as great a mistake to give it too soon as it is to give it too late, particularly a right- or left-turn signal.

It is incorrect to give a slow-down signal when you are turning to right or left. Unless for emergency one clear-cut signal is sufficient and does not confuse.

Assume you are on a road which has many intersecting cross-roads. You intend to turn left or right, into a road which may be three or four intersections away. Should you signal *too soon*, traffic behind you naturally thinks that you intend turning at the first intersection and not at the third or fourth, as you have in mind.

Also remember if you have given a signal to turn, prior to arriving at a cross-roads which is controlled by traffic lights, and then been held up at the light, the wise thing is to give a further signal prior to setting off again at green. The reason is that traffic conditions have changed, due to the time you have waited.

Signals by hand at a roundabout are often neglected by a beginner. Again, a beginner often gives a left-hand signal when about to enter a roundabout; this is unnecessary as one *must* turn left. If the intention is to turn right *on* the roundabout, then a right-hand turn signal should be given. Alternatively, where a roundabout is in the centre of roads which have five or more entries and exits then a hand signal should be given to indicate exactly where you desire to leave the roundabout.

An important hand signal is the "slow-down". It is more important to give this signal between the "lights" than at the

ZEBRA CROSSINGS

Vehicles parked on the "opposite" side to approach side.

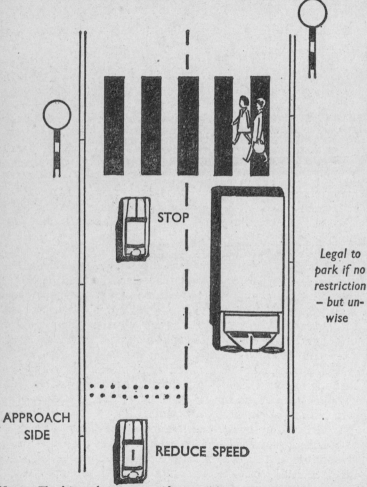

STOP

Legal to park if no restriction – but un- wise

APPROACH SIDE

REDUCE SPEED

Note:—*The driver of car on nearside at position 1 cannot see person stepping onto zebra crossing owing to the large parked vehicle obscuring the view.*

"lights". At a red light everyone expects you to stop. Should you slow down or stop between the "lights" it is unexpected, therefore it is more necessary to give the signal. Particularly this is so on Test. Always signal to the man in the "invisible car" – the car that is not there, yet is always behind you on Test. Some Examiners expect you to signal when approaching a red traffic light – so do so.

What is important is the "slow-down" signal if you are asked by an Examiner (as you will be) to pull into the side of the kerb and stop. Do not wait till you are *at* your stopping point; signal at least twenty-five yards *before* you pull in to the kerb.

Before giving a hand signal make sure it is safe to do so. Look in the mirror first.

There are six times when hand signals should be given. (See page 174.) Irrespective of the gear being used a signal should be given as required. Hand and electric signals (either or both) should be given in top gear prior to taking a left or right turn at a cross-roads. I.e. Check in mirror, brake, mirror, signal position, lower speed, and gear. PERHAPS STOP. Your arm is out giving a turn-right signal and you observe a fast-moving vehicle coming towards you on the off-side. So you cannot make your right turn immediately, therefore change your right-turn signal to a slow-down signal. All drivers should realize that the purpose of a signal is to let other drivers and all road users know what you are going to do . . . not what you are doing.

Learners often signal indicating their intention to overtake a parked vehicle. This is necessary only if a definite detour is being made, and not if your car is positioned to overtake in plenty of time. You can anticipate your overtaking and bear out gradually checking in your mirror. Signal only if car at rear is near or travelling fast, and do it by hand or indicator as the Examiner requests. *Do not prolong signal of this kind.*

Whilst on Test, indicators can be used in conjunction with hand signals (especially *left* indicator). You may be asked to give one type and later the other type only.

IMPORTANT: On Test if using hand signals (sometimes requested) the instruction "turn right" should be done as follows: Check in mirror; if safe to do so, arm out of window with palm facing oncoming traffic (this signal is to indicate your intention to take up a crown of the road position) when there, return hand to wheel and change-down a gear. Immediately after the change-down *again* indicate Right signal and keep your arm out until you are about to make your turn. You *must* have two hands on the wheel when turning.

HALT SIGN and TRAFFIC LIGHT SIGNALS

When approaching and preparing to stop, always give direction signal *first* . . . if a "slow-down" signal is needed when you are between vehicles give it after the directional signal. If using hand signals repeat direction signal just prior to moving off. When turning left (even if using hand signals) the left indicator should also be used.

HAND SIGNALS

When pulling in to the kerb for the purpose of parking in a straight forward position (or normal kerb stopping) give the hand signal meaning "I intend to slow down or stop". (See page 174.) It is incorrect to use a mechanical or flashing indicator for this purpose. Neither do you give a pulling in or turning left signal.

GREEN TRAFFIC LIGHT FILTER ARROWS

If left and right arrows show at the same time, you can go left or right, *but not straight ahead*.

SIGNALS FOR OTHERS

You are, of course, also tested for the careful heed you give to signals from police and other road users.

CHAPTER FOURTEEN

Three-Point Turn
(BETWEEN PAVEMENTS)

Do not regard this as a method of turning in a Major road. The purpose of a "Three-Point Turn" is to demonstrate to the Examiner that you are capable of controlling a vehicle in a restricted space. Suppose you took your car to a place used for parking. You park and yours is the only car at the time. When you return you find it surrounded by dozens of cars. So, by a series of "shunts" (movements backwards and forwards in first gear, then reverse), you try to leave without taking the paint off other cars.

Should you succeed you have demonstrated your ability to control a car in a restricted space. Under Test the Examiner is not aware of your ability to do this : therefore, you are taken to a narrow street and asked to turn round between the pavements, using forward and reverse gear alternately. If your car wheels strike or mount the pavement during this manoeuvre it is obvious that you cannot control a vehicle.

Understand that if you succeed in turning round between the pavements without striking the kerb, and have taken a *five-point* turn instead of a three-point turn, you have executed the turning as per the Examiner's request. There is a vital difference, however. An Examiner is more impressed by a neat three-point turn, if the street is wide enough to allow this.

The vehicle is drawn in to the kerb-side and halted. You pull on the hand-brake and go into neutral. Starting in first gear, you whip the steering wheel round rapidly and complete a full wheel-lock *as soon as possible*. This causes the vehicle to turn towards the opposite pavement. When the complete wheel-lock has been obtained you hold the steering wheel tight and move very slowly towards the opposite pavement.

It may be necessary to "slip the clutch" (i.e., do not allow the pedal to come up completely). This controls the speed at which you will travel; it is most important to travel AT A SNAIL'S PACE TO EXECUTE THE THREE-POINT TURN DECISIVELY. As the bonnet of the vehicle is nearing the opposite kerb you swing the steering wheel round in the second (or opposite) wheel-lock. This second wheel-lock swings your front wheels to the opposite direction, so that, as you come back in reverse to the opposite pavement again (the one you started from), you are automatically placing the vehicle in a position which enables you to get back to the correct place you want to be. The back of the vehicle should now be about two feet from the opposite kerb (the pavement you started from). Now start off in the first gear again for the completion of your turn.

This explanation is not as complicated as it appears. Remember, on the return journey in reverse you must swing the steering wheel back to the opposite wheel-lock. This must again be executed rapidly, waiting until the back of the vehicle is nearing the pavement (i.e., the kerb you started from at the commencement of the three-point turn) to which you will now be travelling in reverse gear. By going into this lock you are now *correctly positioned* for the take-away, in the opposite direction to that in which you were when you first pulled in to the side of the pavement to commence your turn.

The method as outlined is based on the requirements needed to correctly make a three-point turn in a narrow road. Where the road is wider the same manipulation is required, but it will not be as necessary to get so *rapid* a wheel-lock change, as is required in the narrower road. When the road is narrow it is essential to travel slowly but to think and act quickly in going towards the opposite kerb, during the first part of the three-point turn, remember under Test it is more essential to stop the car before striking the pavement than it is to complete the second (or opposite direction) wheel-lock. Should it be necessary to stop the car rather than strike the pavement, it is imperative (for the correct manipulation of the vehicle for eventual positional purposes) to complete the second (or opposite) lock, immediately and as rapidly as possible, on the return journey in reverse.

Where the road is *very* narrow : when going forward in the first completed wheel-lock at the start of the three-point turn, the second (or opposite) wheel-lock should not be started until the front wheels are approximately two to three feet from the pavement towards which you are travelling. Then go into a rapid wheel-lock change. The bonnet of the vehicle must be as straight across the road as possible, even slightly overhanging the pavement. What matters is, keep the wheels off the kerb. Snail's speed and clutch control are the secrets.

Often an otherwise good three-point turn is spoiled by going into this second (or opposite) wheel-lock *too soon*. You must wait for it. If you go into the second lock too early, the nose of the vehicle is carried too far down on the off-side of the road, so your car will be on a slant, instead of as nearly straight across the road as is possible. Exactly the same thing applies during the second part of the three-point turn – when you are coming back, in reverse. Wait until the back of the car is approximately two to three feet from the kerb.

The following sequences may be easier to follow:

(a) Set off slowly in first gear, turning the wheel-lock rapidly, travelling towards the opposite pavement.

(b) As the car nears the opposite pavement swing the wheel-lock rapidly back, i.e., in the opposite direction. Stop the car before it strikes the pavement.

(c) Return to the pavement (from which you started) in reverse gear. If the second wheel-lock has not been completed, do so now, *immediately* you set off in *reverse* gear. Now, as you pull *left*, look *right*.

(d) Hold this second lock until approximately two or three feet from the kerb from which you originally commenced the three-point turn.

(e) When three feet from this original kerb (you are in reverse gear) go rapidly into the opposite wheel-lock. This lock will now turn your front wheels to the position required for completion. Stop the car before the rear wheels strike the pavement.

(f) Start away in first gear towards the opposite pavement. Because you got your correct wheel-lock before stopping this last time, the car will move towards your off-side. You have now completed a correct turn.

THE THREE-POINT TURN

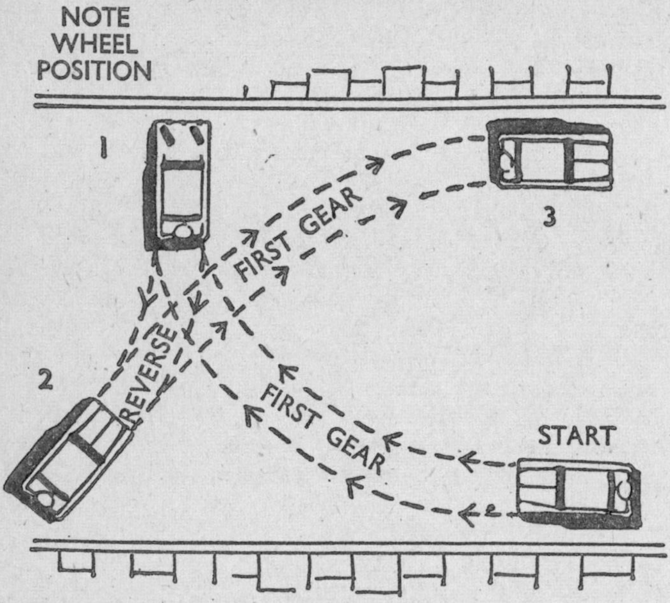

DIAGRAM 4

At point 2, wheel position is changed to opposite lock. Check continuously for safety.

A three-point turn can be of great use should you find yourself in a cul-de-sac. See diagram No. 4.

ALL THE TIME BE SURE TO WATCH FOR DANGER.

Many are failing on Test while doing this manoeuvre because they are not doing everything in a methodical and considerate manner.

COMMON FAULTS

Incorrectly putting gear-lever into neutral *before* the hand-brake has been applied . . . always hand-brake first.

Not looking right and left *before* setting off.

Not applying hand-brake immediately on stopping. Always apply hand-brake immediately you stop. (Dia. 4, (1 and 2).) This is almost always necessary owing to the camber at the edge of the road. Without the hand-brake you would be likely to hit the kerb. A common fault is not continuously checking for safety during the three-point turn.

Gear Changes and Double De-Clutch

THE beginner should remember it is necessary to go up and down the gear-box AS OCCASION DEMANDS. Often on Test a learner will use the gears unnecessarily, or alternatively not often enough. The author appreciates that gear-changing can upset a beginner, and due to this, mistakes are frequently made. Correct use of gears comes eventually through practice and experience, but, as pointed out in Chapter Two the formula quoted will be of great value. This chapter is meant for an entirely different purpose. Chapter Two explains how and when; Chapter Fifteen explains *where*. You are driving along a straight, busy road, and there is a stream of traffic travelling steadily at 25 m.p.h. You are the eighth vehicle in the stream behind number one. For some reason, unknown to you, the traffic is losing speed. Because of this you, too, must slow down. First raise your toe off the accelerator pedal; you will then lose speed and the speedometer needle will fall accordingly. When the speedometer falls to 15 m.p.h. you slip into third gear.

You will still be travelling with the traffic, at 15 m.p.h. instead of 25 m.p.h. Traffic is moving slowly and shows no sign of picking up speed, and your speedometer needle falls to 10 m.p.h., so you go into second. Next you notice the traffic is moving quicker. You now gently depress the accelerator and your vehicle begins to pick up. The speedometer reaches 15 m.p.h. or so, therefore you change up to third gear. The traffic is again on its way, building up to 25 m.p.h. As before, you again squeeze the accelerator-pedal gently and your speedometer will soon touch 20 m.p.h. Slip into top and build up to 25 m.p.h. to enable you to keep in your position. So it continues, gear changes up and down, *as occasion demands*.

There is the time when you are climbing, which necessitates a change-down from four to three or perhaps three to two, dependent on gradient or individual vehicle.

Again, the wise driver should make a practice of going down the gear-box when travelling down a hill. The beginner sometimes uses the foot-brake instead of the gear-box when descending. This is not good for the brake linings, nor good driving. It is also dangerous as the car is less easily controlled; *using the lower gears downhill creates engine resistance, thereby giving greater car control.*

I have often been asked by learners if third gear can be engaged from fourth, if one has left it too late, when going downhill and the vehicle is gathering speed. It can. A modern synchromesh gear-box may be used safely without the need to double de-clutch. You can go from fourth to third gear at almost any speed, providing always the clutch-pedal is depressed first and is not allowed to come back quickly. The higher the speed when such a change-down is made, the more essential it is to *control the upward movement of the clutch especially if going downhill.* This must be released smoothly and evenly. To engage second gear from third under similar conditions, it is strongly recommended that the speed be reduced by gentle application of the foot-brake, to 10 m.p.h.

For the benefit of those who cannot double de-clutch and wish to do so, here is a simple explanation. (Double de-clutching is not normally necessary in a modern car with synchromesh gears.)

DOUBLE de-clutching: (Going up). First gear to second gear – press down clutch pedal, and at *same* time de-celerate (foot *off* accelerator), slip gear into neutral, release clutch, again press down clutch and slip lever into second gear, and once more release the clutch pedal gently and then accelerate. It is the same procedure from second to third and third to fourth.

DOUBLE de-clutching: (Going down). From fourth gear to third or from third to second ... Off accelerator, press clutch-pedal, slip gear-lever into neutral and clutch *up*, then accelerate and off accelerator immediately, then clutch *down*, and lever into third, clutch-pedal *up*. The greater the speed of travel ("during a change-down" double de-clutch), the greater the amount of acceleration required. Here is an itemized version for going down to simplify the double de-clutch.

1. Off accelerator
2. Clutch-pedal down
3. Gear-lever into neutral
4. Clutch-pedal up

5. Accelerator down and up
6. Clutch-pedal down
7. Lever into lower gear
8. Clutch up

NOTE: At number 7, if double de-clutching on a synchromesh it is advisable to slip lever into lower gear just as the acceleration is dying down. But *not* with the old type of vehicle which has the "gate-change" gear-box.

It often happens, especially on Test, that a rapid change-down is essential to prevent engine stalling. You are approaching traffic lights and have changed to third, to be on the safe side – as you get near, the red and amber lights change to green; a car in front "dithers" as it is taking off and you get a little panicky. Instead of "standing" on your foot-brake at this crucial moment, you should get down smartly into second gear. By the time you have done so the chances are that the driver in front will have got away. Because you have now engaged second gear, you also will be in a position to accelerate gently and proceed.

There is an expression, "Gassing in the gear". This means that with the synchromesh gear-box of the modern car, when going down from four to three and three to two the method used for changing a gear is as follows:

You are in fourth and intend a change – to third. The clutch is pressed down and the gear-lever put into neutral. You then accelerate briefly, as the increased "rev" tone dies away slip the lever into third. The clutch is then allowed to come up smoothly. Apply the same procedure when changing down from third to second gear, with just a slightly stronger "rev" (more acceleration) for three to two, than for four to three. Also remember that the greater the speed of the car the more "revs" you need (more acceleration in neutral).

You should not engage first gear from second gear if the vehicle is moving; UNLESS YOU ARE PRACTICALLY AT A STANDSTILL OR FIRST GEAR IS SYNCHROMESH.

The foregoing applies only when going down, not up, the gear-box; its primary purpose is to prevent a grating of the gears as the gear-lever is moved into position. In the modern car double de-clutching is hardly needed: indeed the novice who may find it difficult can dispense with it until he has more experience and change by the ordinary method. *After all thousands now driving and driving well, do not know how to double de-clutch or gas-in gears!*

On Test one could gas-in the gear only when changing down *uphill*. This prevents loss of road-wheel speed and creates more pulling power.

NOTE

If using a three-forward speed gear-box on Test one should always start away from a standing start in first gear; unless the car is facing downhill, when a second-gear start is permissible. It is wiser to start in first gear with a four-forward speed box also (unless it is a high-powered car). If facing up a hill *always* start in first gear.

CHAPTER SIXTEEN

The Pre-Selector Gear Change

THE "WILSON" Pre-Selector gear-box fitted to some high-priced cars allows the driver to select the gear he desires to engage (up or down) at any time before actually changing gear. It is incorrect *ever* to use the gear-engaging pedal as an ordinary clutch pedal.

With a "NEWTON" automatic clutch there is no clutch-pedal for it is engaged automatically by accelerating the engine and disengaged by taking the foot off the accelerator in a similar manner to the Fluid Flywheel.

The Daimler Fluid Flywheel transmission device takes the place of both the clutch and the flywheel of the ordinary car's transmission. In fact the Daimler Fluid Flywheel and Pre-Selective gear-box are *both together* in the Daimler car. Others have used Daimler patents under licence.

A Pre-Selector change is not self-change, as the pedal is the change lever. The Fluid Flywheel is a form of clutch and the "drive" is the fluid (oil). Do not confuse fluid flywheel with the Pre-Selector gear-box.

The gear-lever is dispensed with and its place is taken by what is known as a "quadrant". This quadrant is usually found on the steering column immediately underneath the steering-wheel proper. A component part of the quadrant is the Pre-Selector arm, and this is the lever which is used to *select* the desired gear. On the quadrant is marked the numbers of the gears and the position of neutral.

We will now take the vehicle on a run. You start up. It is wise to check if the Pre-Selector arm is neutral. As there is no visible indication of the gear which might be engaged (or neutral for that matter) you should *depress* the gear-changing pedal and quickly release (*after* the Selector arm has been placed in the neutral position), to ensure that it is, *in fact, in neutral.* Not that this would make any great difference to your eventual "getting away". The purpose is to eliminate any excessive drag (oil drag), which would place a great strain on the starting system. This would be in the nature of an excessive load, and would be less desirable in the colder months. Be positive that your hand-brake is at the *on* position.

Incidentally, one can, if one wishes, depress the gear-engaging pedal, then select number one on the quadrant and release engagement-pedal. But the following is the correct method.

Assume you have selected number one; the engine is running, so you now depress the gear-engaging pedal and release *quickly*. To release slowly would cause unnecessary wear on the gear driving bands and eventually these would be worn out. You then take off the hand-brake and accelerate very gently. (I feel it is advisable to point out that if the slow-running petrol jet is set for *more* than slow-running purposes, then the car would begin to move away in gear perhaps before you anticipated it.) The car will now move forward in first gear.

When it is in motion you can select second-gear, move the Pre-Selector arm into number two position and then *rapidly* depress the gear-changing pedal and instantly release. Whilst you are depressing this pedal your foot must be *off* the accelerator-pedal. Again accelerate gently and the car will move along in second. Note, the car will not move away in the new gear until you accelerate. To engage third and fourth gears in turn you repeat the procedure. It is the same method when engaging reverse.

Remember the gear does not operate until *after* the gear-engaging pedal has been depressed and released. It is the very same when changing down.

Now for a few words on things you can and can not do.

For the Hill-Start, using the Pre-Selector and Fluid Fly-wheel type of vehicle, we assume the vehicle is stationary.

The hand-brake is at the *on* position. Select number one, and depress and release quickly the gear-engaging pedal. Accelerate slightly and then release the hand-brake.

When manoeuvring, e.g. as the three-point turn or reversing, do *not* use the gear-engaging pedal as you would use the old type of clutch. In the old type of pedal, you keep your foot on the pedal for the purpose of "slipping" the clutch, to enable you to have clutch control. With the type of mechanism we are discussing (Fluid Type or Self-Change) it would be disastrous to keep your foot on the gear-engaging pedal, because you would eventually wear out the gear-box bands.

Care should be taken that the gear-changing pedal is *always* fully *depressed* when used. There is mechanical adjustment for the gear-box bands and if the pedal is not fully depressed when being used, wear on the bands takes place and subsequent mechanical failure.

It is possible, with this type of vehicle, to select number four (fourth gear) and then move away from a standing start. If this was attempted on the old type of vehicle you know yourself what would happen. Although this *can* be done on the new type, obviously, it is not recommended.

On the Fluid Flywheel type of vehicle it is correct to be travelling along in number four (fourth gear) and then to *Pre-Select* another gear whilst so travelling. Suppose the car was travelling at, say, 40/50 m.p.h. in fourth gear, and you expected to take an acute left-hand turn, some few hundreds of yards along the road, you could pre-select second gear by medium of the Selector arm on the quadrant, and when you come to your corner, all you have to do is *rapidly* to depress and release the gear-engaging pedal and you would then be in second.

The bus driver does this when he is expecting to stop at a given point. He will select number one while travelling along in top (fourth gear) so that he will be ready to set off immediately he gets the conductor's bell to do so. It will be gathered that you can stop (irrespective of the gear) by merely applying the brake, and you would *not* stall the engine.

With the old type of clutch unit and with the Fluid type you could ask someone to give you a tow, for the purpose of getting away if the battery happened to be low. You could also start your vehicle in gear and run downhill in the above circumstance (low battery). Neither of these methods could be used if your vehicle was the pre-selector type with a Centrifugal Clutch. The reason being a Centrifugal Clutch does not have mechanical connection with the gear-box *unless* the engine is "revved" up.

With this type of car (F.F.W.) you have a powerful method of emergency braking by selecting number one or two (gear) if going down a steep hill. There may be transmission jar, but not the damage to gears which would be expected with the ordinary gear. Obviously, this way of braking is not recommended normally.

If a stop is required one merely releases the accelerator and applies the brakes. The car can be stopped in any gear without risk of stalling the engine (if the mechanism is working correctly).

There is no stalling point because if the "revs" get below a certain number, the engine is automatically disconnected.

Make sure, when you use the Pre-Selector arm, that the notch you wish to use (number 4.3.2.1.N.R.) is *correctly* engaged. If it is not, then the gear-engagement pedal will jump right up (some 8 inches) from the floorboards and of course you are not then in your selected gear. Should this happen, the thing to do is immediately to *stamp down* on the engagement-pedal until it is flat to the floorboards and at once release it, assuming you have in fact correctly selected a gear.

Should the necessity arise for a disconnection of the engine rapidly, such as having to apply the brakes suddenly, you could then use the gear-engaging pedal for this purpose, in the same way as you did with the ordinary clutch.

THE MANUMATIC OR SEMI-AUTOMATIC CLUTCH (TWO-PEDAL CAR CONTROL)

On a Manumatic (Two-Pedal Control Car) you squeeze a small "lever" fixed on the gear-lever. This small "lever" takes the place of the clutch-pedal. When changing gear you accelerate as required. When starting on a steep hill you put the *hand-brake off* as you FEEL the car pulling away. You do everything on this type of car (as you would on a three-pedal car) except control a *clutch-pedal*.

These "one-way" modern answers to the weight of traffic are a God-send, but like many blessings have to be treated with care.

DUAL CARRIAGEWAYS

REMEMBER (if you value your life)

1. Many drivers on first reaching one appear to go quite insane and increase speed out of all proportion to safety. Don't do so and be on guard (watch in your mirror) for the madmen who do.
2. Driving on them is in many respects similar to driving on *motorways,* or *one-way streets* (see appropriate pages).
3. Keep alert, don't let your eyes wander from the road. Watch for signs that the dual ends and the return to two-way starts. *Forgetting one has returned to two-way is the cause of serious accidents.*
4. An inexperienced driver can be so startled by being passed by a 100 *plus* m.p.h. car that he may swerve, possibly into death ! Therefore keep to the centre of your lane and watch in your mirror for what may be coming up on you. Always *know* what is behind.

After going fast for a long way the inexperienced are apt to approach the *terminal* roundabouts at suicidal speed. These are probably the two most likely causes of accidents on motorways.

CHAPTER SEVENTEEN

Fully Automatic Transmission

THERE are different versions of the fully automatic transmission systems such as the electro-magnetic drive and the Borg-Warner Model 35 which latter system has been specifically designed for medium-sized cars.

The Borg-Warner Model 35 is a Fluid drive and operates ideally on *all* gears. It is suited to a four cylinder engine and provides unique top-gear flexibility as well as exceptional fuel economy at low road speeds.

The application of this transmission, say, to the B.M.C.'s 1622 c.c. engine ushers in a new motoring experience to many motorists. Driving motions are cut by as much as 70 per cent.

Being the only automatic transmission for medium-sized family cars which include a "park" position on the selector, it offers great advantages as a trailer-towing equipment, i.e. caravans, etc. Model 35 also provides for a "push-start" in the event, for example, of a flat battery.

Cars fitted with this type of transmission have two pedals only and a Selector, mounted on the steering-column, provides park, reverse, neutral, lock-up, and normal drive, positions. For all normal driving, control of the car is exercised through the two pedals. A novice would find it difficult to stall the engine – and a "hill-start" becomes a dream.

DRIVING THE CAR

For normal motoring the drive position is used and the gear automatically changes from first to second and second to third depending upon road speed and accelerator position. The gears change in the reverse order upon reduction of vehicle speed. Down-changes may also be effected from third to second and second to first by "kickdown" pressing the accelerator-pedal down to floorboard) provided that speeds are below the pre-set maxima.

In "Lock-up" position, the car starts from rest in first gear and remains locked in this gear with maximum engine braking until the driver selects "drive" position when the gear will automatically change to that suitable for the speed of the car. Should this speed be suitable for second this gear can also be held by immediately moving the selector back to "lock-up".

If "Lock-up" is selected at speeds up to 20 m.p.h. an immediate down-change to first occurs and the transmission will remain locked in this ratio with maximum engine braking, for descending steep hills, etc. At speeds over 20 m.p.h. an immediate down-change to second occurs; appropriate engine braking is provided and there is no up-change. If speed is then reduced to below 10 m.p.h. the transmission will automatically down-change to first gear and remain locked in this ratio. This ratio can also be obtained at speeds up to 20 m.p.h. by "kick-down". In this way it is clear that the driver can completely over-ride the automatic operation. The makers recommend that "lock-up" should not be selected at speeds in excess of 55 m.p.h.

The Borg-Warner Model 35 Automatic Transmission has many features other than the unique flexibility, the torque-convertor (force ... pull ... twisting) operating in all gears provides top-gear performance down to 12-14 m.p.h. Further, it needs no periodic maintenance or adjustment: it is "fluid-filled, for life" and it has provision for "rocking" – alternate selection of "D" and "R" (drive and reverse) extracts the car from mud, snow or sand.

TIPS

"P" (Park) ... The transmission is in neutral and the car is mechanically locked against movement should the Selector be moved to "P" accidentally. If stopped on a hill it is advisable to apply the hand-brake. Always move the lever to this position when the car is parked. The engine may be idled or run for tuning in this position.

"N" (Neutral) ... In this position the car may be coasted, towed, or pushed. Do not move the Selector to "N" when travelling at speeds above 40 m.p.h. Always move the lever to "P" if it is necessary to use the starting-handle.

If necessary to tow the car for any reason whatever, this can be done when "N" (Neutral) is selected.

If battery is flat, with this type of car, it is much safer to call in a garage break-down service – unless the starting-handle does the trick.

Moving Away from Rest

Start engine, move lever to "D", accelerate, release hand-brake. As speed of car increases intermediate and then direct top-gear will be engaged progressively and automatically. Thereafter all ratio changes will be made to suit the car speed and torque demand.

"Kickdown"

When a sudden burst of acceleration is required to pass another car, or extra power is needed to climb a hill depress the accelerator as far as possible beyond the full throttle position. The transmission will then change down from direct top to intermediate and remain there until the accelerator is released or until loss of engine revs causes stalling. "Kickdown" does not operate above, say, 50 m.p.h. If a long climb is anticipated or prolonged use of low ratio is necessary manual low should be used and engaged when the road speed is below, say, 30/35 m.p.h.

Reverse

If the Selector (lever) is moved to "R" (Reverse) while the car is travelling forward at more than 3 to 5 m.p.h. the effect is to change into neutral ... and a reverse interlock prevents the engagement of reverse above these speeds.

Stopping

Stop the car in the normal way by applying the foot-brake, leaving the control-lever at "D" until the car is stationary; move the lever to "N" or "P" and apply the hand-brake. As an example, stopping at traffic lights or at a Halt sign there is no

OVERTAKING

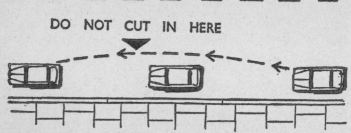

If clear in front and behind, come out GRADUALLY. When over-taking, be at least three or four car lengths ahead and check in mirror over left shoulder.

need to move the control from "D", but it is necessary to hold the foot-brake and prevent the car from moving if the accelerator should be accidentally depressed.

Starting up hills from stop: –

If the car is parked on a hill with the lever at "P" it may creep slightly downhill against the brakes so that the parking pawl becomes tightly engaged. To free the transmission apply the foot-brake lightly, slightly depress the accelerator, and release the hand-brake; engage reverse if the car is facing downhill (or move the selector to "D" ... if facing uphill). Depress the accelerator slowly until the pawl is heard to click out of engagement and *immediately* apply the foot-brake *fully*. The car should not move during this operation; it may then be driven away.

Soft Road Surfaces (extracting vehicle from mud etc.): –

"Rocking" the car. Hold the accelerator-pedal so that the engine speed corresponds to a road speed of 3 to 5 m.p.h. and move the selector-lever *quickly* from "R" to "L" and back. It is important to move from "L" to "R" while the car is moving forward, and vice versa. If the forward speed rises above 5 m.p.h. no reverse will be obtained, since the reverse interlock will operate.

CHAPTER EIGHTEEN

Steering, Double White Lines, Etc.

THE most important thing to remember in steering is the position of the hands on the wheel. All drivers do not hold the wheel in the same way. There is the school of thought which maintains that "ten-to-two" (as on the clock) is the best. Others that "two-forty" is right. I believe the "east-to-west", or the "quarter-to-three" position is ideal. This gives an equal distribution of balance, is comfortable and allows for easy manipulation. No matter which position you decide upon, you should never cross the hands on the wheel.

The driver who "wraps" his arms over the wheel is incorrect. Test Examiners just don't like it. If I were to have a person on Test who "crossed" his hands on the wheel, he would not pass. It is bad driving and largely swank. To drive with the elbow resting on the open window ledge is also taboo.

The wheel should not be gripped tight as if your life depended on it. To hang on like grim death, moving the arms with the wheel, as one would riding a bicycle or a motor-cycle, is also wrong. You should hold the wheel lightly but firmly and allow it to slide through the hands, pulling the wheel to right or left as direction indicates, but *not* pushing it. Do not allow one hand to "ride" with the wheel. If pulling the wheel down to the left, loosen the right hand (release the grip) and let the wheel slip freely. Vice-versa if pulling to the right.

This pulling of the wheel is a series of short, continuous, smooth movements, neither jerky nor erratic. The beginner often feels nervous, but it would help to REALIZE THAT, AFTER ALLOWING FOR THE LITTLE PLAY ON ALL STEERING WHEELS, ONE INCH OF "PULL" (ACTUAL STEERING PULL) IS ALMOST THE EQUIVALENT OF TWELVE INCHES OF STEERING DIRECTION TO THE FRONT ROAD WHEELS. Therefore, when steering on a straight road very little "pull" is required to alter course. When the wheel is gripped tightly and the arms stiff, it results in a tense feeling, the driver steering as if a handlebar movement were being executed. This causes the vehicle to swerve in different directions. *The more lightly the wheel is held, the easier it is to steer.* On taking a left-hand bend the wheel is turned in left-hand pulls, and when round the corner the wheel commences to "unwind", it should be helped to a straight steering position by pulls of the right hand.

Steering through traffic is a question of judgement as to distances between vehicles, and must come by experience. Beginners often "wander" and it is most noticeable when a hand-signal is being given or when a gear is being changed. These are the two occasions on which the wheel should be held less firmly and *the eyes kept "on the road"* (not on the gear-lever) whilst an effort is made to keep straight. (See diagram 5, page 75).

It is essential to *practise* steering with one hand because there are times (e.g. using gears) when one has to do so. Learn to avoid "Wandering" because only one hand is used. Looking down or away is the chief cause and wandering can mean death.

Don't take left-hand corners so closely that your back wheels hit the kerb. This damages tyres and possibly wheels and axle. But don't go so wide that a cyclist (not realizing you are turning left) can be "caught".

Learners often find difficulty in steering in reverse, particularly if executing the reverse into a narrow opening. This manoeuvre is one which must be done correctly on Test, and will be discussed in Chapter 19. When reversing forget left and right turns and remember that in the forward gears the front wheels pull the back wheels, whilst in reverse the front wheels push the back wheels. All steering is controlled through the front wheels.

Do remember there are blind spots caused by the framework of your car – at the front as well as the back. When reversing be careful not to hit children or low vehicles (e.g. motor-cycles) which may not be visible.

This *right* method of using the steering-wheel may be easier to understand if the learner adopts a *stroking* movement. With the right hand *stroke* the wheel from, say, quarter past the hour

DIAGRAM 5

SUGGESTED HOLD FOR STRAIGHT DRIVING

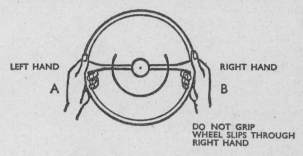

LEFT HAND   RIGHT HAND

A   B

DO NOT GRIP
WHEEL SLIPS THROUGH
RIGHT HAND

METHOD SUGGESTED WHEN TURNING LEFT OR RIGHT

Each time the left hand pulls down left it is immediately returned to position 'A' for the next pull. When turning right the procedure is obviously reversed. I.e., Pull with the right hand at the same time releasing the left hand. When the turn has been made, the wheel is then pulled the other way for the purpose of straightening up. In many cars, self-centring assists this process.

NOTE. *The primary intention of diagram 5 is to emphasize how* INCORRECT *it is to 'cross' hands on the steering wheel.*

down to twenty-five minutes past, and take hand back *immediately* for commencement of next *stroke* down. Use left hand in the same *stroking* movement alternatively, i.e. down ... and up ... down ... and up.

TYRE BURSTS

Tyre bursts these days are rare but if one does you must react quickly ... *they can be frightening* ... Grip the wheel tightly and do your utmost to keep the car on its proper course. In a front wheel burst the car is apt to sway over to the side of the burst. Try to avoid braking (which tends to throw the car further over) and strive by steering to avoid hitting anything until the car comes to rest. FOR SAFETY, REPLACE WORN TYRES.

DOUBLE WHITE LINES

This system is based on European standards.

The double white lines consist of the continuous white line with a second line, continuous or dotted, close to it. These lines have been put down where visibility ahead is so limited that it is always dangerous, in one direction or both, to encroach upon the offside of the road.

The rules are simple and the same as in all countries in Europe which use them. Where there is a DOUBLE WHITE LINE a driver must not cross or straddle the CONTINUOUS line if it is the line NEARER to HIM. The driver must obey the indication of the CONTINUOUS line on HIS side of the road. Arrows are marked on the road preceding each continuous line directing drivers to the left.

It is an OFFENCE to ignore the ruling. See Highway Code (page 160).

WARNING LINE

Single white lines will be of two kinds only, both of them broken.

First of all there will be the line which is intended as a warning to drivers that it may be dangerous to encroach on the far side unless they can see the way ahead is clear. This consists of a broken white line with small gaps and it will be used where visibility is restricted, but not sufficiently to justify a complete ban on crossing. Crossing the broken line will not be prohibited, but motorists will be well advised in their own interests to heed its warning.

LANE LINES

The second kind of dotted line has long gaps between strokes. This is the line which all motorists know; it is used on straight sections of the road to divide the traffic into lanes.

Gradually the present single continuous lines will disappear, to be replaced by whichever of these types of line is the more appropriate.

ONE-WAY STREETS
(In Towns/Cities)

Many of these appear weekly; and because of narrow streets, parking and jay walking pedestrians congestion is acute.

Often car speed is reduced to a crawl and 10 m.p.h. is common. On Test this means much 2nd gear use and perhaps 1st. Be ready to give a gentle toot on horn and ready to get both feet down unexpectedly.

When turning right in these one-way streets get over to off-side kerb as soon as possible.

Regard the off-side kerb (3/4 feet from) as the "crown of road position" used in ordinary road/streets ... when turning right.

If your turn right at a cross-road out of this one-way street is into a street which is another one-way street, watch for traffic coming across from your *left*. But, if traffic is *coming from your right* wait until it is safe to proceed. It depends upon which direction traffic is flowing in the one-way street you are soon to enter.

Do not forget your mirror and signals.

YELLOW LINES (AT GUTTER)

No doubt in time these will spread to towns and villages throughout the U.K., especially where roads are narrow. In London (where there are many) the single one means *no parking* during restricted hours of parking; the double line, *no parking day or night* (otherwise vehicle is removed).

CHAPTER NINETEEN

Reverse into a Narrow Opening or "Limited" Opening

ON Test you will have to reverse into a narrow opening. Do not confuse this with the reverse you may be expected to demonstrate should the Examiner ask you to change your direction whilst you are travelling along a major road. This latter will be explained in Chapter 21.

The chief purpose of the narrow opening reverse is to see if you can control the vehicle carefully and correctly in a public parking place. When parking the attendant may tell you to reverse your car between two others. It would be bad driving were you to scrape the wings.

Therefore, under Test an Examiner does not take you to a public parking place as he does not know if you are competent. You will go where a substitute for the two cars (one on each side) can be utilized. That is a narrow opening. This may be an alleyway where there are pavements on either side; it may be a gateway between two iron pillars, or a passage between buildings with no pavements.

The object is to reverse your car absolutely into the centre, between either the gateposts, the walls, or the pavements. It is in order if necessary during this reverse manoeuvre to stop if you see that you are not steering correctly dead centre; then to pull out again in forward gear to "straighten up". You would then be in a better position for your reverse into the opening. But – and it is a big but – as in the three-point turn, the psychological factor is identical. The Examiner is impressed by a performance of complete steering and vehicle control ending in your car going straight into the opening at the first attempt without any half-in-and-out-and-in business.

Should it be necessary for you to come out with a view to straightening up, do not go back to the original starting-off point but drive straight forward out of the opening some two or three yards at the most. Do not under any circumstances pull out into the street beyond the crown of the street. Make sure the roadway is clear. (See Diagrams 6 and 7, pages 80 and 82).

After much thought I offer a method whereby it should be possible to execute this reverse manoeuvre first time, right in the centre of the opening. The idea is to have an equal amount of clearance on each side. It would not matter greatly if there were two feet on one side and one foot on the other. It would not be so good to have two and a half feet of clearance on one side and six inches on the other.

Practise this manoeuvre till you can do it repeatedly from either side of any narrow opening about eight feet wide. On Test you will be asked to pull into the near-side of a street a few yards this side of a narrow opening. The Examiner will ask you to take up your position for the purpose of demonstrating your ability to reverse into the opening.

The position for this manoeuvre is vital, *approximately three to four feet from the edge of the kerb*, preferably four feet away than two feet. (See Diagram 6). It is essential to place the vehicle as parallel as possible to the kerb. You do not want four feet from the kerb with the near front wheel and two feet with the near rear wheel.

You should be one car length beyond the opening.

It is usually regarded as easier to do this reverse from the right, that is, with the pavement on the near-side (the kerb near the driver's seat). The reverse from the left is thought to be more difficult because the width of the car is between the driver and the kerb. Some Examiners are satisfied with one reverse, the one on the difficult side; others expect a reverse from either side. We will assume the "ideal" position has been taken up for the reverse from the easy side.

In reverse, for short distances, have car control by "slipping the clutch". Most beginners do not appreciate that if a vehicle engine is correctly "tuned" it will travel forward or reverse on the flat by merely allowing the clutch to come up slowly and smoothly, without acceleration. To "slip" the clutch means to hold the clutch-pedal with the foot at the place where the vehicle begins to move. In other words, you do not allow the

(*continued on p. 81*)

DIAGRAM 6

REVERSE INTO NARROW OPENING FROM THE LEFT

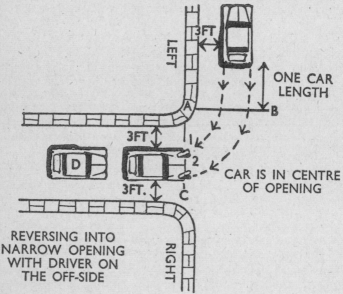

Take up position three feet from and parallel with the edge of pavement. Rear of car to be one car length from the line A———————B.

Steer straight back to the line A———————B, then pull steering wheel to left in a slow continuous complete lock. When car has entered opening and three-quarters of the car is inside opening (with bonnet of car approximately at level with the point C), look through the rear window and unwind steering rapidly in order to straighten up front wheels. (See line A ———————C). Then move slowly back to position D.

Straighten up the position of car between the pavements.

It is most important to unwind at the psychological moment.

If you unwind too early the rear of car will swing to the pavement on the right (inside opening).

If unwind is too late the rear of car runs into pavement on the left (inside opening).

REVERSING ROUND A PAVEMENT

Stop one car length beyond the end of street on the near-side. Now drive in REVERSE round this corner and stop on the near-side about two or three car lengths back from the corner. You will often be asked to do this when your car is facing downhill. Thus you have to do a hill-start in reverse. (See Chapter Nine.) The slower this reverse is done the more competent it will be.

When finally stopping the car, it should be parked as near to the near-side as possible and the entire vehicle parallel with the kerb.

You are not allowed to drive forward again (after finally stopping) for the purpose of straightening up. It's got to be done while reversing.

Commence this reverse as shown in Dia. 8, but instead of steering the car into the centre (as shown in Dia. 8) ease car gently towards near-side pavement looking through rear window. Line up near-side of car with kerb edge looking away back. Travelling very slowly. Do not be afraid to steer back near-side of car INTO kerb edge. This easing back into kerb is done gradually. When you are about twelve inches from kerb with rear near-side wheels, pull steering-wheel RAPIDLY the opposite way and stop. If you practise it is easy. Do not be afraid of hitting the kerb, but go very slowly and don't hit it.

---

clutch-pedal to be completely released – you *hold* it. This enables you to travel very slowly and gives time to think. Practice will repay.

You are now "slipping the clutch", travelling slowly in reverse towards the opening. You should previously have glanced through the driving-mirror also in front and all round you to make certain it is safe. The kerb-edge is in your range of

DIAGRAM 7

REVERSING INTO A NARROW OPENING WITH THE DRIVER ON "THE NEARSIDE"

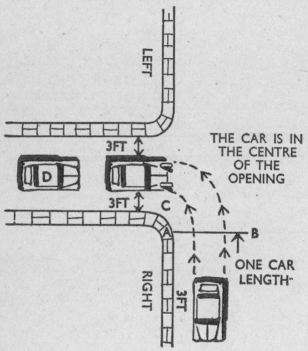

Take up position three feet from and parallel with edge of pavement. Rear of car to be one car length from the line A————————B.

Reverse to opening looking through near-side window. When rear of car appears to be parallel with line A————————B pull steering to right in a slow continuous complete lock. Unwind rapidly at point C, and straighten front wheels, then continue in reverse to position D.

To execute the reverse correctly from the right side of open-ing it is imperative to swing bodily round in your seat and look through the rear window as you are unwinding.

Do not unwind first and turn in your seat afterwards (or vice versa). Unwind and turn in your seat simultaneously.

---

vision as you turn your head looking back towards the opening. The steering is kept straight.

Now you must be very careful, you are nearing the crucial moment, the exact moment, when you go into your wheel-lock. The beginner usually makes the mistake of travelling beyond the near end of the opening which will come first into the range of vision. He is apt to go into the wheel-lock too late owing to the fear of hitting the kerb. Occasionally the wheel-lock will begin too early, then the kerb will be mounted. Should the wheel-lock be made too late, the vehicle will run too close to the pavement or wall on the side nearest to the passenger's seat, not dead centre, which is the aim.

When you get the end of the wall or gatepost level with the end of your car (for our purpose here, the end of the car, is the *rear* wheels ... *not* the rear bumper), the time for going into the wheel-lock has arrived. When looking through the *side* window for *this* reverse, turn your head so that you can also take into vision the pavement on the side you are manoeuvring on. Make sure there are no children or dogs. You have been watching the curve of the kerb and travelling slowly in reverse with the kerb as your guide, and when it is time for going into the wheel-lock you may think you are going into it too soon. This, however, is an optical illusion for if you do not go into the lock soon enough it will be too late. Therefore, as the rear of the car appears almost level with the end of the opening, driving slowly, you go into a slow-continuous complete wheel-lock. (See Diagrams 6, Page 80, or 7, Page 82.)

As you reverse into the opening a complete wheel-lock is essential. At this stage, as the rear of the car has entered the opening and a good half of the car also, say up to the point where the driver is on the turn, as it were, it is imperative, for success, that the driver turn fully round in the driving-seat, his back to the door and looking through the rear-window.

Many learners make the mistake of looking only through a side-window, or, worse, steer the car in reverse while looking towards the bonnet. Because the car is travelling in reverse steering direction is lost, with the result that the car mounts the pavement, or goes to one side, or is steered into the opening in a zig-zag manner.

Remember the main purpose of this reverse is to demonstrate your ability to control the car in a restricted space. Under Test conditions Examiners expect you to continue your reverse into the opening and travel until asked to stop. You may be allowed to halt after you have gone two car lengths into the opening or four or five lengths, dependent on the desire of the Examiner. Merely to reverse part way into the opening and stop would be incorrect.

Most Examiners wish to be assured that after the car is placed correctly into the opening, it can be steered properly in the reverse direction, maintaining a straight course. That is why I stress the necessity for the learner to turn well round in his seat at the psychological moment and look through the rear-window. Let me put it to you this way: you would not drive along any road in a forward gear and at the same time turn your head and look out of the rear-window. Therefore IF TRAVELLING IN REVERSE YOU SHOULD NOT BE LOOKING ANYWHERE BUT IN THE DIRECTION OF TRAVEL.

You are now at the critical point, having turned in your seat and approximately a good half (rear half) of the car in the opening. At this stage it is essential to synchronize your movements. As you turn in your seat to look through the rear-window you must pull the steering-wheel round also into the opposite wheel-lock. *This straightens up the front wheels.* Now look backwards (through the rear-window), fix your eye on some object in the distance, or, if a lane, the centre of it and, as you reverse the car, aim to centralize your position with the distant target as your objective. It will in most instances be necessary to alter the steering slightly to the left or right to keep your car in the centre. (Unless asked to keep near the edge.)

I have found that where a learner has difficulty in maintaining a straight course whilst in reverse the adoption of the following method has succeeded. Forget right and left during reverse steering; regard the vehicle as having four corners. Draw an imaginary line down the centre of the car, from the bonnet through the car, between the driver's and the passenger's seat, and on to the rear-window. You will now have your half of the car and the half at the other side of the imaginary line. You also draw an imaginary line through the steering-wheel, from "north" to "south".

There are now two corners of the car on your half, and two corners on the other half; in the same way, the complete off-side of the car (your half) and the complete near-side of the car (the passenger's half or other side of the imaginary line) *will be controlled by the corresponding half of the steering-wheel.* So the left hand on the steering-wheel controls the near-side half of the car and the right hand on the steering-wheel controls the off-side (driver's side). (This applies equally in forward gear).

Therefore, in reverse it is a question of where you want a particular corner of the car to go. If you want the rear near-side corner (the passenger's side) to go to the left you pull left on the steering-wheel. In other words, WHICHEVER DIRECTION YOU WISH A PARTICULAR CORNER OF THE CAR TO GO, THAT IS THE SIDE YOU PULL THE STEERING-WHEEL. If in a forward gear you intend to take a left-hand turn you pull on the left-hand side of the steering-wheel. Very well, if in reverse do exactly the same. Left – pull left; right – pull right. It is as simple as that.

To reverse into the narrow opening from the left (the difficult side), the side which places the driver away from the kerb, you still take up the "ideal" position. As you start to travel backwards (having checked through your rear window first) your head is turned so that you can see through the rear portion of the near-side window, having an eye range of the pavement towards which you are travelling, the portion of side-window which you look through will be practically immediately above a point where the rear near-side road wheel would be. Again the optical illusion. As the corner of the wall or gatepost comes into view through the near-side window, and when (the back end) of the car appears to be level with the corner or post which first comes into your range of vision, *now* is the time to go into the wheel-lock. NOTE : – The bracketed words (the back end) for our purpose, i.e. for this particular reverse manoeuvre – is where the rear wheels are, NOT THE REAR BUMPER BAR.

You drive slowly, going into a slow-continuous complete wheel-lock, and as before, when a good half (rear half) of the car is in the opening, you move yourself bodily round in the driving-seat and AT THE SAME TIME pull the steering into the opposite lock and straighten up the car between the pavements, or posts as you go straight back. You are *now* looking through the *rear* window. The golden rule during this reverse; *there are no medals for speed.* You want to move slowly, smoothly, correctly, and straight into the opening, dead in the centre first time. It needs a lot of practice.

It might be mentioned here that if you have to park your car in a small space between two other cars it is always much easier to do so by driving alongside the front car and reversing into the space, rather than trying to drive in, in a forward gear. If the space is very limited it is frequently impossible to get close enough to the pavement except by reversing. (See Diagram page 87.)

GUM BOOTS AND THE LIKE

NEVER drive in gum boots. They can slip off the accelerator or get stuck under the brake-pedal forcing the accelerator on! An almost sure way to get killed.

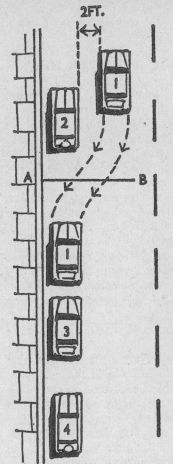

PARKING BETWEEN CARS

Do not try to park in an impossible space. Drive No. 1 car alongside No. 2 and be about two feet apart. Stop when the rear wheels of No. 1 are level with the middle of No. 2. Check through the rear window and reverse slowly by "slipping" the clutch. (The pace should be that of a snail.) Pull the steering wheel slightly left (left hand down) as you ease back. Keep checking as you enter (for clearance and traffic) into the vacant space. But do not get too near No. 2 ... one foot away is safe. As the rear of No. 1 is moving slowly into the vacant space, increase left-hand wheel-lock. As the rear of the car nears the kerb edge, change quickly to a right lock, making sure that your front is clearing the car in front. This straightens up the car. Prior to your complete stop, again pulling the steering LEFT ... not too much ... to straighten up the front wheels. This may need several manoeuvres.

Then move forward to the line AB so that you occupy the middle of the available space so as to leave room for others to get out. This manoeuvre is now often required on Test.

CHAPTER TWENTY

Reverse into a Narrow Opening on a Hill

IF your car is facing uphill and you have to reverse into a narrow opening from that position great care must be taken. Often a candidate on Test will run back too quickly and shoot past the opening, or will try to go into the opening too fast. Either would be incorrect and he would fail.

Everything is the same as in Chapter 19 except for car control method, which is as follows: —

AS THE HAND-BRAKE IS RELEASED THE FOOT-BRAKE IS USED to hold the car on the hill. The clutch-pedal is also held down and the gear is in reverse position. Keeping the clutch-pedal down, you slightly release foot-brake to allow the car to run slowly down the hill towards the opening. Immediately you have done so you slowly release the clutch until the gears engage (you can "feel" the urge of the car to move away). But do not completely release the clutch-pedal – hold it. (See Chapter 6 on Clutch Control).

You then secure perfect control and will then be able to proceed at your own speed.

Alternately, if the rear of the car is up the hill you must adopt the method explained in Chapter 9 on "Hill-Start". (The procedure is identical except that in this instance the car will be travelling in reverse). Also remember in connection with the reverse into the narrow opening on Test: —

You may have an Examiner who is particularly keen. He may tell you to pull up and stop the car after you have driven beyond the end of the "limited opening" into which he wishes you to reverse. When that happens you have missed the opportunity to take up the "ideal" reverse position (as previously quoted and shown in Diagram 6). To attain perfection here it will be necessary to "swing" the rear of the car "out" (see Diagram 8), as not knowing why the Examiner wanted you to stop, you will be too close to the kerb.

Should the narrow opening only be a gateway, or between posts, or an opening where the pavement does not continue into the opening itself, then the manoeuvre requires a little different technique. Here is an infallible method.

Take up our "*ideal*" position. Instead of driving straight back to end of wall or corner, *aim* rear corner of car (corner *nearest* to gatepost) and endeavour to *wrap* car *round* this near post, i.e. *miss* post with rear corner of car by about six to twelve inches. Let car glide slowly into opening and steer carefully into centre.

REVERSING UPHILL

When reversing *uphill* and car is moving slowly off (you are still "slipping" clutch) gradually allow the last half inch of pedal to come up, giving *added*, gradually *increased* acceleration to get the car up the hill. Now remove foot from clutch-pedal but hover over pedal. For steeper hills steadily increase acceleration.

THE FAULTS OF THE WEEK-END
OR INEXPERIENCED DRIVER

The professional driver has seen scores of accidents and perhaps dozens of people killed or injured. The 5,000 miles a year driver may have seen few SO LACKS THEIR UNCONSCIOUS EFFECT ON HIS DRIVING. It is hardly his fault if he is not an expert. People fail to realize that in the first 50,000–100,000 miles one is but learning.

The professional normally feels safe on Monday to Friday but hates to drive at week-ends. Many will not take the risk. The position is as bad as that. May I set down the chief troubles.

1. The *driver* must be unselfish. His passengers can enjoy the scenery, his eyes must never leave the road area. Many week-end drivers look around them.
2. Talking to passengers. One sees a lot of this resulting in dangerous driving. The *inexperienced* drivers (the majority of week-end drivers) are not advanced enough to drive instinctively and talk at the same time.
3. Wandering over the road, presumably while not concentrating. A common fault.

DIAGRAM 8

REVERSE INTO A NARROW OPENING WHEN CAR HAS NOT TAKEN UP "IDEAL" POSITION

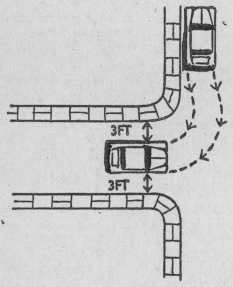

(See diagrams 6 and 7 for "ideal" position)

4. The "Don't you dare pass me" attitude is frequent. Such drivers often swing out to block the passing car. Even if they were correct in thinking they ought not to have been passed, *as a result of their action* many innocent people might be killed. I refer to those who may be in an oncoming car. *Who among us would like that on our conscience for life?*

5. All drivers who can should visit the West End or City of London on a week-day and watch the experts. Nowhere in the world is the standard of competence and courtesy so high.

6. Speed can kill. Remember the expert racing driver who was killed on a public road. Avoid over-confidence or "showing-off".

CHAPTER TWENTY-ONE

Changing Direction on a Major Road

YOU are on Test and driving on a major road. The Examiner may ask you to "change your direction". Many fail to do this correctly; yet it is not at all difficult. All you do is to drive beyond a side street on the near side (the side of the road on which you are travelling) and reverse into this side street, so that you will be facing the major road and in the correct position for changing your direction, that is going back down the road you were previously going up.

Remember you do *not* take a left turn and reverse into the major road. Neither do you do a three-point turn in a major road. Nor do you cut across the major road and then reverse into a side road on the off-side.

When reversing into a side street from a major road for the purpose of "changing your direction", do not confuse this with the reverse into the narrow opening. Each manoeuvre demonstrates a different procedure. One is to judge "parking" ability; this is for "changing direction". When "changing direction", your completed "reverse" position should be as if you had just completed the reverse round a pavement, and parked at the kerb edge. Now check in mirror, and, if safe to do so, signal your intention to move into the crown of road, so that you can take up your position for the intended right-hand turn.

CHAPTER TWENTY-TWO

Left-Hand Turn

IT will be noticed from the items listed on the Test failure chit that one can fail for taking an incorrect left-hand turn – by a "swing out", or, a "wide turn". There are two types of drivers who take a "wide" left turn. The first takes the corner at too great a speed. Because of this the driver knows that if he takes the corner correctly, his speed will make him travel well beyond his near-side, i.e. over the white line which determines the centre of the road he is entering. He could, therefore, easily be upon the off-side of the road he enters, on a left-hand turn; particularly if the road he is entering is narrow. In an endeavour to keep to his correct place on the near-side, he "swings out" on the corner to enable him to pull in again.

The second type of driver may be travelling quite slowly, but due to an erroneous impression he "swings out" on a left-hand corner. He errs because he thinks that if he takes his corner correctly his rear wheels will run over the edge of the kerb. I must point out that although we refer to a street *corner*, there is in fact no such thing. Corners are "rounded" to meet the requirements of modern traffic. The person who "swings out" to prevent his rear wheels mounting the corner does this under a misapprehension. Of course a bus or huge wagon requires space to manoeuvre and could more easily mount the kerb with the near rear wheels.

Who determines a correct left turn? The correct way is laid down by the Ministry of Transport, and interpreted by the Government Testers. The following method I have found to be most successful, basing it on hundreds of successful Driving Test passes. (See Diagram 9, page 94).

When you take a left turn at a cross-road you are joining the traffic stream travelling on the road you are to enter, and this stream will be going your way. Therefore, it is not compulsory to stop unless this junction has a Halt sign or lights against you

DIAGRAM 9

THE LEFT-HAND TURN

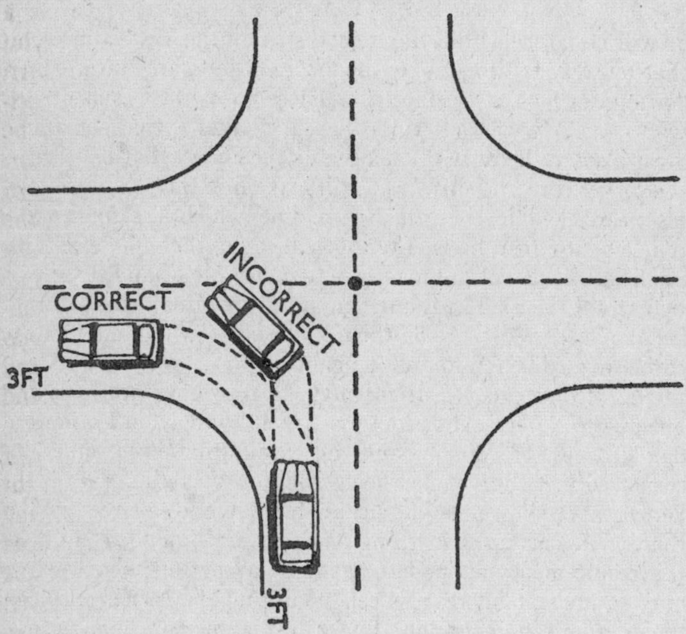

NOTE. Make sure that there are no cyclists on your nearside.

or if an oncoming vehicle is too near for your safe entry. The bonnet of your vehicle should be turned (parallel with the pavement) towards the left. (See Diagram 9).

Any left turn should be taken as follows:—Approximately 75 yards from your left turn, check carefully in driving-mirror, signal your intention and slip into third gear (if there is a three speed gear-box, at about 50 yards from the corner you change down to second gear). Take up position for the turn (three feet from kerb) and brake gently to reduce speed, especially for a "blind" left turn. If you are going uphill speed will be automatically reduced if you raise the foot off the accelerator. The important thing is *second gear for a blind left-hand turn* and third gear for a left-hand turn which is not blind. Should the vehicle have only three forward gears second gear will normally do.

Having got down to the appropriate gear you then concentrate on guiding the vehicle round with both hands. You do not again signal, say, a yard or two from the corner; a left-hand signal should again have been given *between* third and second gear-change, and completed 12 to 15 yards from the corner.

When turning left you look right; that is where danger (if any) is most likely. It must be emphasized the quick look right for safety's sake, should not cause you to forget you are turning left, so whilst looking to the *right and left* you must remember to steer the vehicle to the left: also WATCHING THAT NO CYCLIST HAS COME BETWEEN YOU AND YOUR NEAR-SIDE PAVEMENT.

Beginners are often so absorbed looking right on a left turn that the steering is forgotten completely, or should I say, momentarily, with the result that the vehicle goes straight forward or a very wide turn results. Either of these shows inexperience or just bad driving. As you turn hold the car parallel to the kerb, perhaps a yard out, but do *not* swing out just before turning – as so many do.

When making a left turn which is blind, acute or sharp, do not be afraid to reduce speed. Position early, three feet from pavement, drive straight forward until nose of car appears to be level with edge of pavement (corner you are going round); your speed can be as low as three to five m.p.h. (for Test purposes);

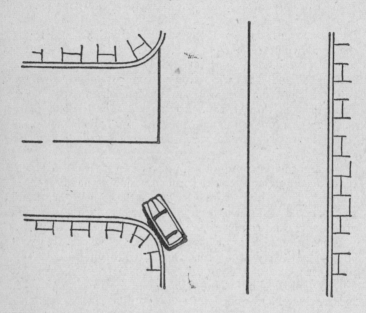

Happens easily on a left-hand turn. May seriously damage tyres or axle or even a pedestrian's foot!

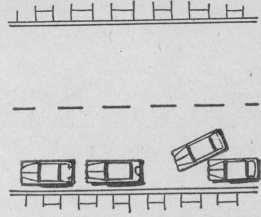

A very common accident. The back bumper or mudguard damages a parked vehicle. Take care when parking but the best thing to do where possible is to reverse carefully into the opening.

then as you check right, pull steering-wheel carefully to left, following pavement all the way round. Remember to unwind as you straighten out. Once round the corner, accelerate and get on your way. Do not loiter in the lower gears when it is safe to proceed. Do NOT exceed 30 m.p.h. in a restricted area.

A difficult circumstance could arise as you get near the corner because of slow moving traffic in front of you, or traffic coming from the right which could mean a complete stop for you or a quick change-down to first gear. If the latter, you could *tail* in, if safe to do so, and move slowly round the corner. If unsafe to proceed do not be afraid to stop. If stopped on a level road and ready in first gear, the foot-brake will suffice to hold the car whilst waiting for a quick get-away. If there is no chance of a quick get-away then apply the hand-brake. Never attempt to beat anyone to it.

CHAPTER TWENTY-THREE

Right-Hand Turn

CORRECT positioning before turning is vital. Incorrect positioning can lead to a Test failure or worse. One must take up the correct position for a right-hand turn *at the correct time.*

Assume you are travelling at 25 m.p.h. and a right-hand turn is soon to be taken. You are about five or six feet from the near kerb. Approximately fifty yards from your intended right turn, look in the mirror and again at thirty yards. Drop to third gear (second, if three forward gears) at 25/35 yards from the right-hand turn. Check in mirror again and take up a crown of the road position IF SAFE TO DO SO. Once you have taken up your position in the crown of the road (for your right-hand turn), you must maintain it. Do *not wander back to the left* nor allow any vehicle at your back to crowd you out of your right-turn position.

If you are about to turn right and you notice another vehicle in your mirror, a lot would depend on the distance he was behind and at what speed he was travelling, as to what to do. If the car was travelling at *your* speed and was eight or nine car lengths behind, you would signal your intention and steer over to the crown of the road, thereby compelling the driver behind to come up and overtake you on your left (near-side). Later in this chapter I indicate the procedure for a different situation.

Keep to the crown of the road, positioning the vehicle so that the off-side, is running parallel with the cat's-eye studs and maintain this position just inside the studs, on your half of the road, until you arrive at the point where you should make your right-hand turn. (See Diagram 10).

You are now in the lower gear, and have extended your right arm, for your signal the arm should remain in signalling position until you are just about to make the turn, when you then bring the hand back to the steering wheel for the purpose of guiding correctly round.

DIAGRAM 10

THE RIGHT-HAND TURN

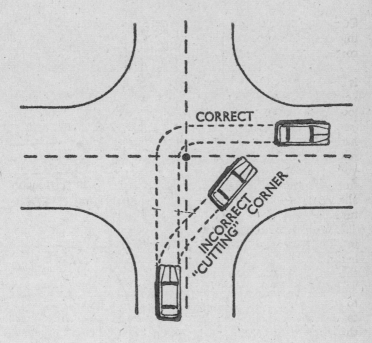

DIAGRAM 11

THE RIGHT WAY TO TURN RIGHT

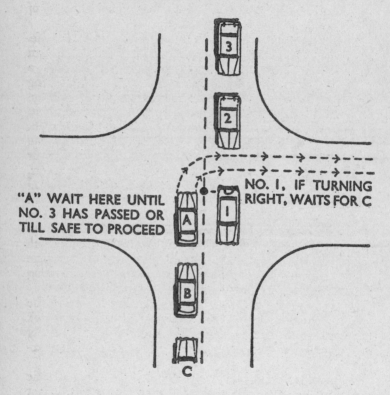

"A" WAIT HERE UNTIL
NO. 3 HAS PASSED OR
TILL SAFE TO PROCEED

NO. 1, IF TURNING
RIGHT, WAITS FOR C

If two cars intend to turn right at a cross-roads when travelling in opposite directions they should pass each other at the imaginary flag-pole in the centre OFF-SIDE to OFF-SIDE.

Ninety-nine drivers in each hundred are unaware of the one right way to execute a right-hand turn at intersections or cross-roads.

It is incorrect to signal and then bring the arm back and put it out again as you get near the point where you intend to turn. One continuous signal is better than two or three short ones, and is less confusing. (See page 53.)

It is futile and dangerous to drive up to five or six feet from your turn and suddenly give a right signal. *Signal in plenty of time.*

Do not take up a crown of the road position until it is safe. Reduce your speed, check in your mirror, and if not sure, turn your head so that you can see that no danger will arise as a result of your taking up a crown of the road position. Having done so, drivers going in the same direction and intending to go straight ahead may position themselves to pass on the left. Remember, cars are fast today. They come up at 80 plus m.p.h. Begin to get into position in plenty of time. BE SURE NO ONE IS IN THE ACT OF PASSING YOU and so not visible in your mirror owing to its "blind" spot – a frequent cause of accidents.

If cars are passing you, give slow-down signal, reducing your speed even to a crawl or stop. When safe, you then tail behind, and take correct position for your right turn. *Once you have gained your position* near the crown of the road, keep your right arm out of the window which should compel traffic behind to overtake you on the near-side (left) if they wish. That is the chief purpose of the crown of the road position when intending to turn right. It is often safer to use your indicator!

Many have failed for incorrect right-hand turns. The common offence is to "cut" your corners. (See Diagram 10). It is incorrect to turn as shown in Diagram 12. This usually happens when an inexperienced driver does not know the procedure.

When taking a right turn remember that if oncoming traffic is approaching the intersection, it is your duty, although not the law, it is *Test* law, to wait in the centre of the cross-road (see Diagram 11) and then continue when clear.

It is also incorrect to turn right as shown in Diagram 13. Why it is wrong should be obvious; by taking up a position nearer the near-side as in Diagram 13 you are tempting a vehicle

DIAGRAM 12
AN INCORRECT RIGHT-HAND TURN

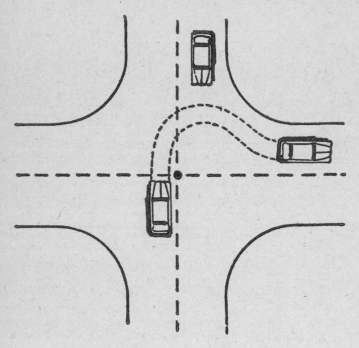

This turn is caused by "creeping" forward.
Do not "creep". WAIT.

DIAGRAM 13

INCORRECT RIGHT-HAND TURN

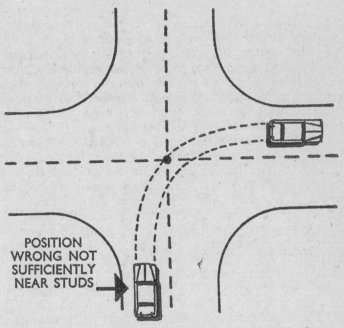

POSITION
WRONG NOT
SUFFICIENTLY
NEAR STUDS

behind you to come up and overtake you on the off-side, at a point where you should be overtaken on the near-side.

I suggest that, for each right-hand turn, you visualize an imaginary flagpole in the centre of the intersection – then go *round* it.

As indicated in Diagram 11 if several cars (going in opposite directions) turn right, it is correct to pass each other *off-side to off-side*. There are, however, a few cross-roads on narrow roads, (e.g. in London) where it is customary to pass near-side to near-side, that is, in front of each other, and extra care is needed. You could experience these on Test.

CHAPTER TWENTY-FOUR

Roundabouts

IT is usual for a Test Examiner to take you to a "roundabout" to satisfy himself that you are competent to negotiate this "One-way" system safely. The purpose of the "roundabout" should be appreciated if you are to drive round it safely. Numbers of young drivers will not remember the days when there were no "roundabouts". They were introduced to cut down accidents at cross-roads and busy intersections: and probably with a view to keeping the traffic stream flowing.

The entrance to a "roundabout" is invariably built "bottleneck" style. This is done to compel the motorist to reduce speed; therefore, on Test the candidate *must* reduce speed, and the wise course is to change down. You change down some twenty yards or so from the "roundabout".

If it is your intention to go round and leave the "roundabout" say, on a road on your right, you should take up a position about two feet from the "roundabout" (see Diagram 14) and *cling* to this position until you are about to make your exit. You should not steer far to the left when negotiating the "roundabout". Neither do you give a left-hand turning signal when you are about to enter the "roundabout". If your intention is to go round a "roundabout", obviously you must be turning right, therefore you should give the hand signal indicating a right turn. Should you desire to go "as the crow flies", you steer towards the centre part of the "roundabout" (position as in 2, Diagram 15), and no signal is required, unless a "slow-down" signal is needed.

Experience has taught me that to negotiate a busy "roundabout" safely and without holding up the traffic, it is best to take up your position in the stream at an opportune moment, never beating anyone to it and always giving way to any vehicle which is nearer than you to any selected spot on the "roundabout" which you must eventually travel over, and which you

DIAGRAM 14
THE POSITION OF A CAR FOR A RIGHT-HAND TURN

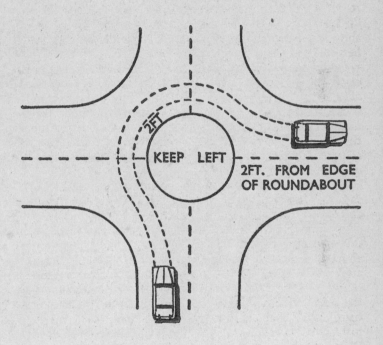

KEEP LEFT

2FT

2FT. FROM EDGE OF ROUNDABOUT

DIAGRAM 15

ROAD 'A'

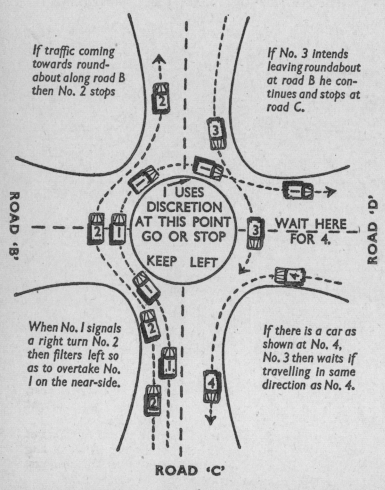

If traffic coming towards roundabout along road B then No. 2 stops

If No. 3 intends leaving roundabout at road B he continues and stops at road C.

I USES DISCRETION AT THIS POINT GO OR STOP

KEEP LEFT

WAIT HERE FOR 4.

ROAD 'B'

ROAD 'D'

When No. I signals a right turn No. 2 then filters left so as to overtake No. I on the near-side.

If there is a car as shown at No. 4, No. 3 then waits if travelling in same direction as No. 4.

ROAD 'C'

ROUNDABOUT SIGNALS

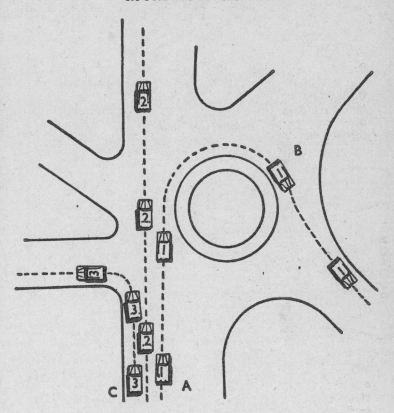

Car 1 gives right signal at A, left at B and, if road clear, moves to the left in preparation. Car 2, as it is going straight on, normally gives no signal. Car 3 gives left signal at C.

Car 2 if turning left at second entrance should signal left at near centre of first entrance on left of diagram. After passing Car 3 on corner watch for traffic coming from first entrance, then ease over to near-side.

have decided is the spot you are making for. (See Diagram 15). It is a question of common-sense and road-sense. Be courteous to other car drivers but not lingeringly so. Do not become an obstruction. Take up your position in the traffic stream immediately it is safe to do so. As you enter a roundabout watch most carefully for anything coming up both on your *left and right*. Roundabouts tend to give a false feeling of safety but if carelessly used can be dangerous, just because drivers think them safe. Study carefuly Diagram 15. TAKE VERY SPECIAL CARE ON DARK WET NIGHTS AT "ROUNDABOUTS".

At some busy roundabouts a "GIVE WAY TO TRAFFIC ON THE RIGHT" experiment is being currently carried out; when you meet this sign, just wait and tail in, when clear to do so.

GREEN – BE CAREFUL

Because the lights are in your favour do NOT assume some Fool or Cad will not shoot through on red and hit you. This is happening more and more recently.

CHAPTER TWENTY-FIVE

D.L.24
(1963)

Road Traffic Act, 1960

Test Centre:

STATEMENT OF FAILURE TO PASS TEST OF COMPETENCE OR OF FITNESS TO DRIVE

(By kind permission of H.M. Stationery Office.)

Name..

Address...

has this day been examined on a vehicle of Group .... and has failed to pass the test of competence/fitness to drive prescribed for the purposes of Section 99 or 100 of the Road Traffic Act, 1960.

Date...........................   ....
                                     Authorized by the Minister of
                                     Transport to conduct tests.

Examiners have regard to the items listed below in deciding whether a candidate is competent to drive. The matters needing special attention are marked for your information and assistance and should be studied in detail.

See "YOUR DRIVING TEST" (D.L.68), Part 2, paras. 1-21.

1. ☐ (a) Knowledge of the Highway Code.
   ☐ (b) Eyesight test.

These numbers refer to the rules in the **HIGHWAY CODE**

CONTROL

2. ☐ Take suitable precautions before starting the engine.

↓

3. ☐ Make proper use of/accelerator/clutch/foot brake/gears/hand brake/steering.
4. ☐ Move off smoothly/at an angle/on a gradient/on level/straight ahead.
5. ☐ Make normal progress to suit varying road and traffic conditions.
6. ☐ Stop vehicle in emergency/promptly and under control.

16, 46, 47

7. ☐ Stop machine in emergency/promptly and under control/making proper use of the front brake.

8. ☐ Reverse into a limited opening either to the right or left/under control/with reasonable accuracy/with proper observation.   16

9. ☐ Turn round by means of forward and reverse gears/under control/with reasonable accuracy/with proper observation.   16

ROAD PROCEDURE   11

10. ☐ Look round before moving off.

11. ☐ Make proper use of the mirror well before
    Take rear observation well before } signalling/ changing direction/ overtaking/ stopping.

12. ☐ Give signals/correctly/in good time/by direction indicators/by hand.   31-32, 41*

13 ☐ Take correct and prompt action on all signals by/traffic signs/traffic controllers/take appropriate action on signals given by other road users.   38, 41-43*
     19

14. ☐ Exercise proper care in the use of speed.   31-32

15. ☐ Act properly at cross roads/road junctions :   19, 37
    (i) proper use of / mirror / signals / brakes / gears/when appropriate.
    (ii) correct regulation of speed when approaching.
    (iii) looking left, right and right again before emerging.   37-38
    37-39, 43-44
    39-40
    (iv) emerging with due regard for approaching traffic;
    (v) correct positioning of vehicle } before/after turning right.
    (vi) avoidance of cutting right-hand corners. } before/after turning left.

16. ☐ Overtake / meet / cross the path of / other vehicles safely.   19-22, 31-40

17. ☐ Keep well to the left in normal driving.	17
18. ☐ Allow adequate clearance to/cyclists/pedestrians/stationary vehicles.	21-27 21-24
19. ☐ Pedestrian crossings/approach at a proper speed/stop when necessary/avoid overtaking at or approaching/avoid dangerous signals to pedestrians.	
20. ☐ Select safe position(s) for normal stop(s).	54-56
21. ☐ Show alertness and anticipation of the actions of/cyclists/pedestrians/drivers.	*See P.174-178

DRIVING EXAMINERS ARE NOT PERMITTED TO DISCUSS
DETAILS OF THIS TEST

GUIDANCE NOTES

1. As already mentioned on the front of this statement, you should make a further study of the pamphlet "Your Driving Test" (D.L.68) in which detailed advice about the test requirements is given. See *Part 2, The Test, paragraphs 1 to 21*.

2. You should also look at the Highway Code rule numbers given alongside the faults which the examiner has marked. Study of the appropriate rules – with Part 2 of "Your Driving Test" – should help you.

3. No further tests on a vehicle of the same Group can be undertaken until the expiry of one calendar month.

4. If you consider that your test was not properly conducted in accordance with the regulations you may apply to a Court of Summary Jurisdiction acting for the Petty Sessional Division in which you reside (in Scotland to the Sheriff within whose jurisdiction you reside) which has power to determine the point. If the Court find that the test was not properly conducted they may order a refund of the fee and authorise you to undergo a further test forthwith.

5. This form should be retained since you may be required to produce it to a licensing authority if you apply for a further provisional driving licence.

CHAPTER TWENTY-SIX

Thirteen Commandments

1. Concentrate on what you are doing.

2. Be courteous to other users of the road.

3. Do not drive "on the horn"; use the horn only when it is advisable to do so, never aggressively but warningly.

4. Signal in plenty of time, clearly and decisively, when needed.

5. Do not stop your vehicle or overtake on a corner.

6. (a) Do not cut in; (b) Give room when being passed.

7. Brake gently, smoothly and firmly, but not fiercely, except in danger.

8. When in doubt, DON'T RISK IT.

9. Never travel faster than you can think.

10. Overtaking can be dangerous – make sure first.

11. Never park in narrow places so obstructing the road.

12. Never take your eyes from the road, or argue with passengers.

13. Stepping on the gas kills more than inhaling it. Better later here than early hereafter !

NOTE :—Most head-on collisions happen when drivers travelling towards each other leave their respective traffic lanes in an attempt to *beat* the man in front, and then find they cannot get back into the lane they have just left.

Cross-roads are also "deadly" places.

CHAPTER TWENTY-SEVEN

Eleven Chief Reasons for Test Failures

1. Failure to answer correctly questions based on the Highway Code and Rules of the Road.

2. Failure to give hand and mechanical signals:
   (a) clearly; (b) concisely; (c) at the correct time.

3. Failure to negotiate correctly a left- and/or a right-hand turn.

4. Incorrectly positioned on the road (especially before turning).

5. Incorrect use of, or failure to use correctly, gears and/or brakes and/or mirrors.

6. For not giving free passage to pedestrians on an uncontrolled crossing.

7. Insufficient experience in traffic.

8. Taking Test before you are ready.

9. Not looking Right, Left, and Right again before emerging at cross-roads and junctions.

10. Speed *too fast* in too high a gear on *approach* at cross-roads and junctions.

11. Failure to exercise due courtesy to other road users.

CHAPTER TWENTY-EIGHT

Your Driving Test

(AS PER MINISTRY OF TRANSPORT LEAFLET D.L. 68 1963.

CROWN COPYRIGHT RESERVED. REPRODUCED WITH THE PERMISSION OF THE CONTROLLER OF H.M. STATIONERY OFFICE).

THE Ministry of Transport has issued a leaflet intended to show the candidate who applies for a Driving Test some of the conditions which must be fulfilled before and during the Test. Some of the contents of this leaflet are set out below for the benefit of those who may not have seen one. Dots (..) indicate passages omitted owing to lack of space.

1. BEFORE THE TEST

THE OBJECT OF THE TEST

However little you mean to drive, if you pass the test you will get a licence allowing you to drive anywhere in Britain ..
whatever the traffic conditions. So the Examiner must be satisfied that you are competent.

A competent driver handles a vehicle safely, displays consideration for other road users, and observes the Highway Code. He also knows the principal causes of skidding, what to do when a skid occurs, and the importance of correct tyre pressures and proper maintenance of brakes. ..

PREPARATION FOR TEST

(i) *Make sure that you get an instructor who really knows his job.*
(ii) Practise over different routes and get experience in traffic. Make sure that you do not cause danger or obstruction to other road users. ..
(iii) Study the Highway Code carefully. ..
(iv) If you live in the country, you should still be ready to answer questions about traffic lights, signs and roundabouts.

APPLICATION FOR TEST

(i) *Apply in good time but do not ask for the test unless you are sure that you are going to be ready.* . .

(ii) An application form for test appointment (D.L.26) may be obtained from any Money Order Post Office or Traffic Area Office.

(iii) Study carefully the table of vehicle groups, and the note immediately above it, on the back of the form. . .

(iv) Give all the particulars asked for on the application. . .

(v) Send the correct fee, £1. If you are being tested on an invalid carriage, motor mower, pedestrian-controlled vehicle or vehicle exempted from duty under section 6(6) of the Vehicles (Excise) Act, 1962, it is only 2/6d, payable to "The Ministry of Transport". . .

(vi) Send in your application at least 21 days before the day you wish to be tested. . .

(vii) Do not wait until your provisional licence has nearly run out.

(viii) Address your application to the Clerk of the Traffic Area in which you wish to take the test. You will find the address on the back of the application form. . .

(ix) If you are deaf and dumb, the fact should be mentioned on a slip of paper pinned to your application (see also paragraph 28) . .

THE TEST APPOINTMENT

(i) . . You will get a card which will be a receipt for the fee and will also tell you when and where you can be tested.

(ii) . . Make sure the date and time are acceptable. If they are not, let the Traffic Area Office know. . .

(iii) Tests are arranged to a strict time-table and punctuality will help you and the Examiner . . Remember that parking may be difficult and allow sufficient time for it.

(iv) In order not to waste your own time, and the Examiner's, make sure of the following points *before you come:* . .

   (a) that your eyesight (with glasses if worn) is up to the required standard;

   (b) that your driving licence is not out of date (not even by one day) and that you have signed it;

(c) that your vehicle carries 'L' plates; and

(d) that your vehicle is thoroughly roadworthy. . .

II. THE TEST

GENERAL

1. (a) Knowledge of the Highway Code

You cannot expect to get through the test unless you have carefully studied the Highway Code. The Examiner will watch whether you put its rules into practice, and will also ask you questions. . .

(b) Eyesight Test

You will be tested on your ability to read (with glasses, if worn) a motor car number plate at the prescribed distance. . .

CONTROL

2. . . Make sure that the gear lever is in neutral and the hand brake engaged before you start the engine.

3. Make proper use of/accelerator/clutch/foot brake/gears/hand brake/steering. . .

Foot Brake. Avoid hurried or harsh use of the brakes.

Gears. Change down in good time, and *before* coming up to the hazard . . Do not look down at the controls. . .

Do not drive for a distance either in neutral or with the clutch disengaged.

Hand Brake. You should know how and when to use it. . .

Steering. Keep both hands on the steering wheel unless it is necessary to remove one to signal or to change gear. . . Steer a steady course. Do not rest your arm on the window ledge. . .

4. Move off smoothy/at an angle/on a gradient/on level/straight.

. . Taking care not to inconvenience or endanger other traffic or pedestrians. . . *It is particularly important that you should be able to co-ordinate the use of the hand brake with the accelerator and clutch.*

5. . . You cannot expect to satisfy the Examiner if, regardless of road and traffic conditions, you drive at a 'crawling pace' in a low gear – or make unduly slow progress.

6. . . Stop vehicle in emergency/promptly and under control . . However quickly you stop, you should try not to

lock the wheels because if you do the vehicle may get out of control and skid. . .

7. Stop machine in emergency/promptly and under control/ making proper use of the front brake (Motor cyclists) . .

8. Reverse into a limited opening either to the right or left/ under control/with reasonable accuracy/with proper observation.

You will be expected to drive the vehicle in reverse gear into a limited opening and to continue to drive it in reverse gear, keeping reasonably close to the kerb, for some distance after you have 'straightened up'. . .

9. Turn round by means of forward and reverse gears/under control/with reasonable accuracy/with proper observation.

ROAD PROCEDURE

10. Look round before moving off . . even though you have looked in the mirror.

11. Make proper use of the mirror well before | signalling/changing direction/
Take rear observation (overtaking/stopping
well before |

. . You must act sensibly on what you see in it. Use the mirror in good time. . .

12. Give signals/correctly/in good time/by direction indicators/by hand . .

When you use a direction indicator, see that it is cancelled as soon as your intended movement is completed.

When you signal by hand, give only the signals illustrated in the Highway Code and give them clearly and decisively.

Even if your vehicle is equipped with direction indicators you will be required, during part of the test, to show that you can give the recognized hand signals. (This does not necessarily apply if you are a disabled driver.)

13. Take correct and prompt action on all signals by/traffic signs/traffic controllers/take appropriate action on signals given by other road users . .

Failure to comply with a 'HALT at Major Road Ahead' sign, for example, will involve failure. . .

14. Exercise proper care in the use of speed .. particularly having regard to the weather and the state of the road.

15. Act properly at crossroads/road junctions:
  (i) *proper use of/mirror/signals/brakes/gears/when approaching.* ..
  (ii) *correct regulation of speed when approaching.* .. At crossroads or junctions not controlled by 'HALT' signs or by stop signals (e.g. traffic lights or police) you should so regulate your speed that you can stop, if necessary, without encroaching on the intersection.
(iii) *looking right, left, and right again* BEFORE *emerging.* ..
(iv) *emerging with due regard for approaching traffic.* .. Be extra careful when entering roads which have bends or gradients.
(v) *correct positioning of vehicle* $\begin{cases} \textit{before/after turning right.} \\ \textit{before/after turning left.} \end{cases}$ ..
If the wheelbase of your vehicle is unusually long (e.g. a lorry) so that in some instances you cannot keep well to the left just before the corner, take great care that you do not trap a cyclist or motor cyclist on your left as you turn.
(vi) *cutting right-hand corners.*
Never cut a right-hand corner. This is a dangerous practice because it reduces your vision to the right, puts you on the wrong side of the road, and leaves insufficient room for vehicles to enter the road which you are leaving. ..

16. Overtake/meet/cross the path of/other vehicles safely .. Always allow a safe clearance between your own vehicle and the vehicle you are overtaking.
Do not overtake unless you are sure that you can regain your normal position on the left-hand side of the road without forcing vehicles coming towards you to swerve or slacken speed ..

17. Keep well to the left in normal driving. .. Do not hug the middle of the road.
18. Allow adequate clearance to cyclists/pedestrians/stationary vehicles. .. When about to pass parked vehicles, re-

member that one of them may pull out or a door may be opened. Allow plenty of room.

19. Pedestrian crossings/approach at a proper speed/stop when necessary/avoid overtaking at or approaching/avoid dangerous signals to pedestrians . .

You must allow free passage to a pedestrian who is using a ZEBRA crossing. At pedestrian crossings CONTROLLED by light signals or by the police, you should give way to pedestrians who are already on the crossing when the signal to move is given.

Do not overtake when approaching a pedestrian crossing.

It is not necessary to wave an invitation to pedestrians to leave a pavement or refuge. In fact, this should never be done unless you are sure that there is no danger from other vehicles.

20. Select safe position(s) for normal stop(s) . .

21. Show alertness and anticipation of the actions of cyclists/pedestrians/drivers . .

If you do not think ahead you will find yourself unprepared for situations. . .

FURTHER GUIDANCE ABOUT DRIVING TECHNIQUE

22. Sequence of Movements in Driving

Try always to remember and put into practice the safest sequence of movements, i.e.

  i. Mirror (or, on two wheels, glance behind).

  ii. Signal

  iii. Manoeuvre.

23. Lane Discipline

Well before you reach a junction, make sure you are in the appropriate lane. Do not switch from lane to lane. . . Do not "jump the queue".

Do not overtake on the left to gain a forward position in congested traffic unless the driver in front has signalled his intention to turn right, or vehicles in the right-hand lane are moving more slowly than you are. . .

24. One-way Streets

When driving in a one-way street, position your vehicle either on the left or the right of the carriageway, depending on whether you intend to turn off to the left or the right.

25. Dual Carriageways

When you wish to turn right off a dual carriageway you should take up a position near the central reservation, well before you reach the opening. You should be prepared to wait in the opening, placing your vehicle so that it does not obstruct traffic which is passing in either direction.

SOME NOTES ABOUT DRIVING TESTS
AND DRIVING EXAMINERS

26. Uniformity of the Test

The test is prescribed by Regulations and every effort is made to ensure uniformity of procedure and of the standard of competence required in order to pass, wherever you happen to live or choose to take the test. The route on which you will be tested will have been selected to provide a fair test of a learner-driver's ability. There is an extensive system of supervision of driving tests which takes several forms. One way in which you may become aware of this is by having a Supervising Examiner in the vehicle when you are tested. If this happens, there is no question of your having to satisfy two people instead of one. Remember rather that the senior official is present in the general public interest. He will take no part in the test but is there to see that your Examiner does his job precisely as the Minister wishes it to be done.

27. The Examiner's Job

The Examiner will be sympathetic but he is not allowed to discuss your driving because that would be bound to distract your attention, and when the test has been completed he must be available to meet his next candidate punctually. Unlike your instructor, the Examiner will not be able to engage in comment by way of encouragement or criticism of your driving. You should therefore be prepared for periods of silence during the test which should not be regarded as implying any dis-approval or unfriendliness. In other words, the Examiner will confine himself to the business in hand which entails directing you over an approved route and asking you to carry out exercises at particular places. It will be useful to remember that he will have a good idea of how you feel because every Ministry Examiner has himself undergone stringent tests in driving.

Listen carefully to what the Examiner asks you to do, carry it out as well as you can . .

28. Candidates with Disabilities

If you have a physical disability you may find the circumstances of a driving test particularly trying. For this reason, the Examiner will be as helpful and considerate . .

If you are deaf and dumb, you may bring an interpreter . .

29. General Condition

The vehicle in which you take a test should be mechanically sound, with controls, seating, and other equipment so disposed as not to interfere with the conduct of the test.

30. Adjustment of vehicles

Vehicles driven on test should not be specially adjusted for the purpose of carrying out more easily such manoeuvres as the reversing exercise. A fast-running engine can interfere with normal control and will involve excessive speed in many situations.

31. Commercial Vehicles

Drivers of light vans or similar vehicles which are fitted with only a driver's seat should bring with them a suitable box or cushion on which the Examiner may seat himself securely.

Candidates should not present themselves for test on vehicles which are loaded or partially loaded.

32. Left-hand-drive Vehicles

If you present yourself for test on a vehicle with left-hand drive you should see that (a) the stop-light at the rear of your vehicle and (b) the mechanical direction indicators on *both* sides of the vehicle are working efficiently.

You should bear in mind that the driver of a left-hand-drive vehicle in this country should exercise special care, including the fullest use of the mirror, when about to overtake, alter course or to turn right . . Be sure you know, and can demonstrate to the Examiner while the vehicle is at rest, all the hand signals shown in the Highway Code.

33. Safety Harness

. . You may wear it during the test, or not, as you prefer.

CHAPTER TWENTY-NINE

Some Questions asked by Examiners

Try answering these. Use the reference numbers.

1. How do you approach Traffic-Lights, Halt sign, junctions?
2. What is the Highway Code?
3. What should you not do when being overtaken?
4. What should you do before overtaking another car, and on which side do you overtake?
5. When should you not overtake?
6. When is it an offence to sound your horn?
7. How many hand signals are there, and what are they?
8. If you wish to turn the car round in a busy road, how would you do it?
9. How would you approach a Zebra or Panda crossing?
10. What precautions would you take if you parked a car at night on your off-side?
11. Have you, as a car driver, the right of way at cross-roads?
12. Under what circumstances would you drive with extra caution?
13. What is the meaning of white lines on the road?
14. If you wish to park your car other than at a parking place what precautions would you take?
15. When should you not use your head-lights?
16. How would you hand signal to a policeman the direction you wish to take?
17. What is the meaning and sequence of the traffic signal lights?
18. If the amber light is showing alone, which light follows?
19. When can you pass the red light?
20. When are you compelled to stop?
21. What is the rule of the road?
22. Where should you *never* overtake on *left*?
23. What are the regulations relating to speed?

24. When can you overtake on the left?
25. What is the difference to a car driver between the hump-bridge and the low-bridge?
26. Why must you halt when ordered to do so by the sign: "Halt at Major Road Ahead"?
27. Which of the road signs is shaped differently to the others?
    (a) What is the shape of this sign?
    (b) Why is it so shaped?
28. What is depicted on the "Hospital" road sign?
29. What is depicted on the "Crossing, No Gates" road sign?
30. What is the primary purpose of the white lines or cat's-eye studs down the centre of a road?
31. What is the difference between broken and double white lines down the centre of a road?
32. Name six occasions when it is imperative that you look first into your driving-mirror.
33. Name three occasions when you must not pull into the left.
34. How would you travel in convoy?
35. What is the correct procedure when turning right?
36. How many days are you allowed in which to produce your driving-licence and a certificate of insurance?
37. Assuming you are commencing a long journey by motor-car and have checked your oil, petrol and water, name the parts you would also check.
38. What would you do if involved in an accident?
39. If you run over an animal, do you report it to the police?
40. Would you find the "Steep Hill" sign at the "brow" of the hill, at the bottom of the hill, or at top and bottom?
41. How would you travel in fog?
42. At what speed would you travel during the day?
43. At what speed would you travel during the night?
44. Besides police, who else has authority to control traffic?
45. What signal would a policeman give if he held you up from behind him?
46. Give particulars of what is shown on the "school" sign?

47. What is the IDEAL distance to stop behind another vehicle at Traffic-Lights, Halt-sign, or in a line of stationary traffic?

48. In a MOVING stream of traffic what is a SAFE distance to be BEHIND the vehicle in front?

49. When can driving become unsafe on a motorway?

50. Why are cross-winds unsafe?

51. What is a clearway?

52. How do you join a motorway?

53. Name some "DONT'S" on a motorway.

54. Can one turn right on a motorway?

55. If you have a puncture or breakdown on a motorway, what do you do?

56. What does a triangle above a road sign mean?

57. How do you overtake a slow-moving car which hugs the centre of a road in the face of on-coming traffic?

58. If driving at *very* high speed on a 3-lane motorway, which lane would you occupy?

(ANSWERS IN CHAPTER THIRTY)

Answers to Questions in Chapter 29

1. With care. Reduce speed. If lights go green keep speed as traffic flow.
2. The Highway Code is a book issued by the Ministry of Transport for the guidance of all road users.
3. You should not accelerate or pull out to the off-side.
4. Give hand signal. Satisfy yourself that it is safe to over-take. Sound your horn if necessary, and after overtaking return to your proper side as soon as possible without cutting-in. Overtake on the off-side except where a system of control which permits otherwise is in operation.
5. At Zebras, Pandas, cross-roads, brow of hill, hump-bridge, double white lines. If vision restricted or if danger to traffic.
6. When the car is stationary, except when necessary on the grounds of safety. It is an offence to sound the horn between the hours of 11.30 p.m. and 7 a.m. (in a built-up area).
7. Six. (Two signals are the same). Details of these are to be found in the Highway Code (on our pages 174-175).
8. Drive past first "safe" turning on your own side, reverse into it, and pull out into the main road head first.
9. Reduce speed and if need change down or stop, giving slow-down signal.
10. Turn the car round so that it faces the direction of the traffic. Make sure the side and tail lights are on.
11. No. If you are on a minor road, give way to the traffic on the major roads at non-controlled points. At controlled points you obey the controller.
12. In wet and foggy weather, in crowded streets, and near schools. And, of course, in snow or icy conditions.
13. Broken white lines that run parallel with the kerb mean "keep to the left". Those across the road indicate the

stopping places for cars at controlled points. Where the road is divided by lines into three or more "lanes", the left, or near-side lane is for slow traffic, the outer for overtaking.

14. See that you are causing no obstruction by leaving your car opposite another vehicle parked on the other side of the road, near corners, cross-roads, pedestrian crossings, bus stops, etc.

15. When the car is stationary, or when driving in a well-lighted street; and if safe when following another vehicle which you do not intend to overtake.

16. Three signals: (1) Turning right (right hand outside the car, palm of the hand facing the radiator).
    (2) Straight on (hand flat against the windscreen, fingers pointing to the top of the windscreen).
    (3) Turning left (right hand flat against the windscreen with fingers pointing to the left).

17. Red light means "Stop".
    Green light means "Go".
    Amber light alone means "Prepare to stop".
    The sequence is red, red and amber, green, amber, then red.

18. Red follows amber.

19. When a separate green "filter" arrow is showing at the same time.

20. When requested to do so by persons in charge of horses or other animals, by traffic controllers, if involved in an accident, halt sign, police, to allow pedestrians free passage on an uncontrolled pedestrian crossing, to allow passengers to alight from or board a tramcar. (Still a few in the world).

21. Keep to the left.

22. On a motorway or clearway.

23. Speed should be regulated so as to be able to pull up within the distance which can be seen clearly ahead;

circumstances and weather must be taken into account. Strict regard must be paid to any speed limits which may be in force.

24. (1) When the car in front signals a right-hand turn.
    (2) On a "roundabout".
    (3) In a One-way street.
    (4) Moving tramcar.
    (5) Green filter-arrow.

25. You go *over* the hump-bridge and *under* the low.

26. It is an offence not to do so.

27. The "Halt" sign.
    (a) Somewhat like the printed capital "T".
    (b) To distingush it from the other signs, but chiefly because in the winter-time, when the wording may be covered with snow, the shape would identify it.
    Note:—All *circle* signs are prohibitive and mandatory.

28. A black shield with a white cross centrepiece.

29. A railway engine in black on a white background.

30. To divide the road in two (one lane for near-side traffic, and one lane for off-side or oncoming traffic).

31. Study this answer on Page 76, dealing with "WHITE LINES".

32. When you are about to: (1) Stop.   (2) Start.
    (3) Reverse.   (4) Overtake.
    (5) Open door to get out of car.
    (6) When turning right or left, especially right.

33. When turning right, on a roundabout, or immediately after overtaking.

34. With a sufficient distance between your own vehicle and the one immediately in front of you to enable a faster overtaking vehicle to get in between.

35. Look in mirror, and if safe to do so, signal your intention, change down, again look in mirror, take up and maintain a position near the crown of the road and finally, another look in mirror, and, if necessary, over shoulder.

36. Five days.

37. Steering, brakes, tyres, lights, horn, windscreen-wiper, mirror, rear reflectors.

38. STOP. *Get and Give* required information, see Highway Code page 185 under heading YOU MUST ... Read this section MOST CAREFULLY; it is vital.

    You will notice, if anyone is injured you must produce your certificate of insurance, *at the time*, to the police or to anyone with reasonable grounds for requiring it. If this has not been done, the accident must be reported to the police inside 24 hours, and the certificates shown to the police inside five days.

    The author suggests: Get name(s) and address(es) of other driver(s) Insurance Co.(s) and as many witnesses as you can. In a serious accident take road measurements. Your insurance certificate also probably tells you not to admit blame. (Even though you think an accident your fault, it might not be).

39. Report to the police inside 24 hours, unless you have given the information required; see Highway Code page 185.

40. Before reaching the point of descent.

41. With head and rear lights on and with care.

42. At a speed which would enable you to stop with safety at all times within what you could see to be clear ahead.

43. At a speed which would allow you to stop safely within the range of your headlights' vision.

44. Road Scouts, person in charge of animals, person in charge of road works (man with red and green flags), or a street crossing controlled by a warden.

45. See page 176.

46. Two children (in a hurry).

47. A half a car length behind.

48. For EACH 10 m.p.h. of speed ONE vehicle length BEHIND, i.e. At 20 m.p.h. TWO lengths behind ... and so on.

49. Accident in front or high speed in cross winds or bad conditions.

50. They can blow car off-course and affect steering.

51. A stretch of road where no stopping is allowed except for emergencies or breakdowns.

DISTANCES BEHIND OTHER CARS FOR SAFETY

One car length for every 10 m.p.h. of increased speed

10 m.p.h. 1 car length

20 m.p.h. 2 car lengths
30 m.p.h. 3 car lengths
(and so on)

52. See pages 169–170.
53. See page 169, Items 70–71, Page 172, items 85–88.
54. No, but see pages 172–173.
55. Get car on the 8 ft. "Hard Shoulder" having previously looked in your mirror and signalled your intention.
56. Warning and information.
57. Toot *gently* and wait till safe to pass.
58. See Highway Code, para. 79, page 171.

SUMMING-UP FOR LEARNERS

My desire in the previous pages has been to present in easily understandable terms an explanation of all the requirements, all the manoeuvres, and all the do's and don'ts which, I assure you, will be essential if you are to pass the Test. Especially difficult features such as the Three-Point Turn and the Reverse into a Narrow Opening I have propounded at great length, my intention being to give you a word-picture in detail. My reason for this is two-fold: first, I do not think there has been, or is, a similarly detailed explanation in print; secondly, I believe that once a learner-driver has mastered the intricacies of the two above-quoted manoeuvres, he will then have gone far towards acquiring the most important feature of car driving (from the ability-to-manoeuvre point of view) – *car control*.

To further emphasize my belief of this, I would draw your attention to the following facts.

The Three-point Turn and the Reverse into a Limited Opening call for and include all the essentials to enable you to : —

(1) Start.
(2) Stop.
(3) Use the foot-brake and clutch.
(4) Use the hand-brake.
(5) Use clutch control (slip-the-clutch).
(6) Travel very slowly.
(7) Use judgement and safety tactics.
(8) Become used to steering control.
(9) Think fast.

(10) Act fast.
(11) Develop confidence.

What more can you ask?

THIS BOOK SHOULD BE STUDIED, PAGE BY PAGE. EACH IN-
STRUCTION SHOULD BE THOUGHT ABOUT.

IN THE FIRST HOURS WITH AN INSTRUCTOR EVERYTHING
MAY SEEM DIFFICULT BUT, USUALLY QUITE SUDDENLY, THE
WHOLE THING WILL BECOME MUCH EASIER — PROVIDED YOU
HAVE DONE YOUR HOME STUDY WELL.

PART TWO

ADVICE TO THE MORE ADVANCED DRIVER

CHAPTER THIRTY-ONE

General Hints

AFTER passing the Test many people imagine that they have finished the job, and everything will be easy. Equally, many drivers who passed the Test a few years ago consider they are equipped to handle their car, and because they may have driven two or three thousand miles a year without an accident, believe themselves safe. After an accident does occur it is usually this type of driver who refers to the other party with the words, "and the fool. ...." You are still learning after 50,000 miles of driving. Remember that. And after 250,000 miles !

It is true that occasions may arise in which a good driver is unable to avoid an accident, but such happenings are rare. When the experienced motorist encounters "the fool" it is nearly always possible for the former to take evasive action and save lives. It does, however, occur to the really experienced driver as he watches motorists that at least fifty per cent of them should not be allowed out alone. It's as bad as that.

During the period when petrol was difficult and when the majority of motorists were commercial travellers or others who used the road a great deal, the standard of motoring rose appreciably; but since 1946, with the return of the pleasure motorist and week-end driver, our roads have become more unsafe than ever.

Much of what I write in the following pages may appear obvious to many, but on so important a matter as the avoidance of accidents, I am sure I shall be excused if some readers feel that parts of what I say are unnecessary.

One of the sad things about car driving is that until a learner has had an accident or a narrow escape, he is apt to underestimate the dangers of handling a lethal machine. It is unfortunate that death is so final, and, of course many an inexperienced driver may *not live to benefit from his first accident*. And remember, that although it may not be your own death, the death of someone else may be involved.

It is most important to remind readers that the driver of a car can never be a sightseer while his machine is in motion. The driver may be tempted by his passengers to look at this scene or that, but HE MUST NEVER DO SO. He owes it first to other road users, secondly to his passengers, and thirdly to himself to *keep his eye on the road all the time*.

I am reminded of a lady whom I was teaching to drive and who noticed a friend on the opposite pavement and probably thinking that courtesy costs nothing proceeded to bow to her, turning her head round and with it her hands slightly. I was just in time to grab the steering-wheel and avoid a tree trunk.

Another general remark which can be made here is to stress the dangers of skidding. It has been my privilege to drive with some of the finest motorists in Europe, and many of them could be described as extremely fast drivers. Driving with these men in wet or frosty weather, we have frequently *been passed*, especially by women drivers, or elderly men who should have known better, and even ordinary drivers too ... when *our car was doing the absolute maximum for safety* on that kind of road condition.

On one 200-mile drive in winter, we were passed by four cars all of which we later found involved in serious accidents.

Do not be tempted to race some other fool possibly to his death. It is difficult to know when to reduce speed, but on wet roads, if the surface is smooth or cobbled, normally anything over 30 to 35 m.p.h. is dangerous. The snow-covered road or one with a skin of ice on it are *far worse*. A skin of ice can appear on a road without snow and normally in such conditions anything over 18 m.p.h. is too fast. There are, of course, exceptions depending on the width of the road and conditions generally. For example, going up a hill is normally very much more safe than going down.

In night driving sometimes a frost may descend on to the

road which cannot be seen even with the head-lights. The only indication is a SLIGHT ALMOST IMPERCEPTIBLE FEELING OF THE CAR SWAYING – if you feel this sign, drop speed to a safe crawl, ignoring what other ignorant drivers may do. Adverse camber is dangerous. You can stop and test the surface with your foot.

While still writing about the general conditions in motoring, I would like to stress the importance of having efficient brakes, and making sure that your steering is in good order. If the powers-that-be would instruct the police authorities to spend their time checking up on motorists' brakes, side and tail lights, and steering, instead of hanging about for hours in wide roads catching parking offenders, I would admire them more.

I am reminded of a man telling me that he was going at 50 m.p.h., when a lorry swung out and in order to save himself he jammed on the brakes and stopped in his own length. This must have been a classic English "understatement" for it is not possible for a car to stop in three yards at 50 m.p.h.

At this speed it is mechanically impossible to draw up in less than approx. 58 yards which is over twice the length of a tennis court. At 10 m.p.h. a car can be stopped in 5 yards, but at 20 m.p.h. it can't be stopped in 10 yards, requiring approx. 13 yards. At 30 m.p.h. it needs some 25 yards. You will notice then, that the greater speeds require much longer in proportion, in order to stop, and this, therefore, brings me to the greatest safety rule of all : —"Never drive at a speed greater than that at which you can stop within the distance you can see is clear."

Another friend once told me that he was driving on a slippery road when a child ran into it. "I jammed on the brakes and the car turned around four times." This is the opposite of an understatement because the greatest skid ever known only turned the car round once !

In emergency, sometimes to avoid an accident you can induce a skid but the ability to do this only comes with experience as does the ability to rectify the skid.

Another likely accident point is cornering in a hedge-lined lane. It is not safe to conclude the road is empty because you might not be able to see anyone over the hedge. Sheep are

NEGOTIATING AN ACUTE BEND

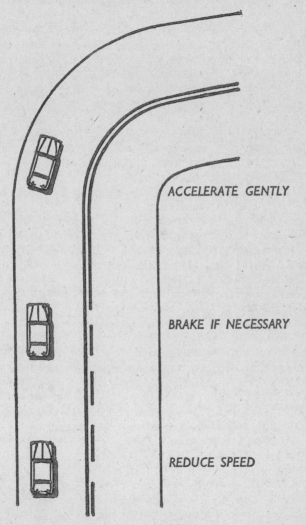

ACCELERATE GENTLY

BRAKE IF NECESSARY

REDUCE SPEED

normally invisible over it and so are children. This also applies to cyclists and motor-cyclists, especially if their heads are down. So corner carefully where there are hedges and SOUND YOUR HORN.

Remember then, most skids occur on corners, therefore, prevention is better than cure, so, Brake *before* you get to the corner, whilst the car is on the straight. Then *gently* accelerate while going round. Do not "roll" round ... and do *not* decelerate. Sudden acceleration is a cause of skidding on slippery surfaces. Also sudden jerks of steering.

BURST TYRES

A burst tyre can be serious. Tyre manufacturers assert that under-inflation is a primary cause of a tyre casing breaking up and then the tyre bursts. Another cause is damage by hitting a kerb. High speeds cause heat – rubber's great enemy. Avoid top speed over long distances.

It is not generally appreciated that the *air* within the tyre *carries the load*, therefore, it is wise to have car tyres inflated to the correct pressure as laid down by the manufacturers.

A regular check on tyre pressures, at least once a week, is advisable, not forgetting the "spare".

Should the rear tyre of a car suddenly burst it is not as serious as a front wheel burst, but in any event the thing to do is to hold the steering-wheel very firmly and endeavour to maintain a straight course.

Obviously, the greater the speed at which you are travelling when a tyre bursts, the greater the risk of ultimate disaster. The essential thing to remember, particularly with a front wheel tyre burst, is to keep the speed of the vehicle the same *after* the burst. Viz :—Do *not* apply the brakes fiercely or immediately. I know that the inclination to do so would be natural.

Try to keep a straight course and allow the car to run itself to a standstill. If the necessity arises to apply the brakes, then do so very *gradually*.

It will be appreciated that when the brakes *are* applied the pressure will be *only* on the wheels which are tyred. Therefore, if the front off-side tyre burst, the application of the brakes would *pull* the car to the near-side, or vice-versa. There is a known case of a front wheel tyre burst, and the wheel itself practically disintegrating; were this to happen hold tight and hope.

Keep tyre pressures right and *wheel nuts tight*.

Although punctures are common, especially if tyres are worn, fortunately bursts are rare. A slow puncture can be caused by a leaking faulty valve/core. While travelling a puncture indication is when steering *seems* to be faulty, the car *veering* to left or right.

"ONE EYE MONSTERS"

Beware the "one-light" driver. You think it is a motor-bike till you are in hospital! The roads at night are full of them and have you noticed how often the defective light is the off-side one, that is, the one nearest you? Be careful with all "one-light" approaching vehicles.

A STARTING HINT

As this is not a maintenance book it is difficult to find a place to include a small hint which has helped so many.

In damp weather if your car will not start try switching on the ignition *while* using the starter instead of before employing it. Personally, I go to the trouble, in very cold weather, of using the starting-handle, before switching on the ignition. I turn over the engine handle about six times. This *frees* the cold and cloggy oil and if you then take the *hint* above you should not have any great starting difficulty. (It is not possible with some cars).

In damp weather leave the bonnet up a few inches; this prevents condensation. If weather is damp and car will not start in the morning try wiping moisture from inside of distributor-cap and also from the terminals. A lot of non-starting in the morning is due to giving far too much "CHOKE". Never give "*choke*" and Acceleration at the *same time*.

OVERTAKING

To overtake efficiently and quickly a car travelling at your speed, especially uphill, check mirror, signal moving out and drop into lower gear, increasing acceleration at the same time.

CHAPTER THIRTY-TWO

More Definite Driving Hints

HERE is some more definite information. In playing tennis the difference betwen the champion and you or me is very often that the expert has made a study of positioning. I want to stress this because I think MORE ACCIDENTS RESULT FROM BAD POSITIONING IN THE ROAD THAN FROM ANY OTHER SINGLE CAUSE. Only a few days ago I happened to see a car driver swinging out of a side road into a main road. In coming out of the side road he had placed his car almost in the centre of the road to allow himself lots of room for the left-hand turn which he was about to take. Unfortunately, a cyclist thinking that he was going straight across rode between him and the kerb only to be crushed a few seconds later. It is true that a lorry or bus has to take a wider corner than a car on account of the distance between the front and back wheels, so the driver must be extra careful to see that no one is coming in on his left.

Another menace is the slow driver who keeps to the middle of the road, instead of well in to the left. A driver may decide to pass him on his inside, which is very dangerous, especially if some other driver decides to pass him on his outside at the same time.

Another of the most frequent positioning faults is in taking right-hand corners. THOUSANDS OF PEOPLE WHO DO THIS BADLY WILL BE KILLED IN THE NEXT FEW YEARS. Before turning to the right you must go on to the right hand side of your half of the road and wait for the oncoming traffic to allow you to go across.

On rare occasions, with heavy oncoming traffic, it might be necessary to edge slowly forward, using any opening (and the horn) thus blocking oncoming traffic so that you can get a clear space to go through. Great care and experience are required. No Examiner would confront a candidate with so severe a test.

Another common fault is that of the inexperienced, who,

instead of taking up the correct position either for passing another moving or stationary vehicle, or taking up position for a right-turn, leaves coming out UNTIL FAR TOO LATE. He is tootling along in his car, then about 10/20 yards before reaching the stationary vehicle, he suddenly swings out. When about to pass or before taking up your position for a right-hand turn the ideal is to move out VERY *gradually*. If possible commence this outward movement over a hundred yards beforehand. This enables those behind to get some idea of your future actions. Remember, emergencies apart, avoid all *sudden* swings either out or in, especially in one-way streets.

It is useful to remember when overtaking that, in the event of having to come back into your near-side sooner than you intended, due to the action of the driver in front (or for any reason whatsoever), it is wise to "sight" the vehicle now *behind* you, in your driving-mirror, *also* take a rapid glance over your left shoulder to see if you are completely clear of the vehicle you have overtaken.

Accidents result from following the car in front too closely. Always keep well behind it and preferably *not* immediately behind but rather to the near-side unless when overtaking. This gives you a chance should the preceding car meet with an accident, lose a wheel as occasionally happens, or brake suddenly. You should be able to stop in time, but if that is not possible, you should be able to clear on either side. This is very important advice.

Many drivers, and especially learners on Test, are often worried because they cannot determine if they are on a priority or major road, where there are no indicating road signs. When approaching a cross-road which appears to have no priority over the one upon which you are travelling, you are nearing what is known as an unobserved cross-road. The thing to do is change-down and look to see if the road you are on "flows across" the other, then you are on the priority or major road. If you are *not* on the priority road you must stop and check. Look right and left then repeat, and if traffic is clear get into first gear and away. Engage second gear before you cross the road; that is, immediately you are moving ... lingering in first is bad driving. Cross-roads are often *serious accident* areas. Always show care.

THE BLIND SPOT

There are, unfortunately, many motorists who do not appreciate the limited range of their mirror. I have seen stationary cars move away after only a glance in the mirror, and seeing nothing, swing out, so causing an accident to a cyclist or vehicle. Similarly, MOVING MOTORISTS often fail to see another car IN THE ACT of passing and swing out. Do PLEASE REALIZE THAT THERE IS A BLIND SPOT ON EVERY INSIDE MIRROR, so you must also look out of your side window, over your right shoulder before moving out.

A mirror on the off-side wing or jutting out from the off-side door jamb, covers the blind spot, and is worth fitting.

BLIND SPOTS

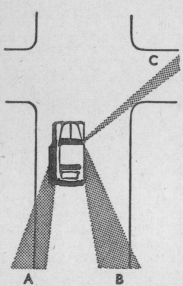

Shaded areas represent approximate blind spots, (A and B) in your centre mirror.

A and B are dangerous if you move out of your lane without checking over your shoulder or in good side-mirrors. C is the corner frame (where such exist) and can be dangerous especially at roundabouts at night for cyclists. Frames obscure drivers' vision, as does a passenger who leans forward or backwards when you are checking near-side. Steamed windows are DEADLY. Clean them.

TURNING RIGHT AT A CROSS-ROAD

Being sure there is no one close behind or passing on your right, take a quick look to the left *prior* to making the *actual* turn when you are on the crown of the road. Your *immediate* danger at this movement, may come from your left.

CHAPTER THIRTY-THREE

The Avoidance of Accidents

SOME readers of this book may be fast drivers and they have to be catered for as well as the slower driver. Indeed, ironically enough, it is sometimes the fast driver who is the safest.

Arguments are frequently found in the Press for and against the use of the horn. Comparisons are made that in some countries its use has been discontinued and the percentage of accidents has fallen. But what applies to one country does not necessarily apply here.

In the United Kingdom, nothing was heard against the use of the horn until the anti-noise campaigners campaigned. Such a fuss did they create that the memory lingers on today; many people think that the horn is not supposed to be used at all. One excellent achievement of this campaign was the abolition of horns between 11.30 p.m. and 7.0 a.m. in built-up areas only. After dark, lights should be used instead of the horn.

But, let it be *clearly understood* that as an accident-preventer, the horn takes precedence even over the brakes. I am not advocating its eternal use, nor "driving on the horn", but when going *round blind corners*, or merely stopping small children from running into the road, it is ESSENTIAL THAT THE HORN PLAYS ITS PART. As a means of preventing people stepping into the road from behind stationary vehicles its use is often required.

In thickly populated areas where a child is playing, or a pedestrian may jay-walk, *it is wise to keep either the finger or thumb near the horn ready to press it*. In an emergency the rule is *press the horn, apply the brakes and clutch*. Critics may say that sometimes the horn will frighten the pedestrian or motorist and this is true. If the pedestrian has seen you and panicked, it is not necessary to hoot. This book allows for common-sense on the part of the reader. Foolish people will not buy it.

HEAD-ON ACCIDENT

In motoring, occasions can arise in which some kind of accident is unavoidable; the lesser of two evils may have to be chosen. *One accident which should always if possible be avoided is the head-on smash.* The alternative to this rule might be where one had to run amok on to a pavement full of people, in such an instance it might be better to choose an honourable death for yourself.

The following also should be remembered. In the event of your near-side front wheel striking the kerb (particularly at high speed) a great danger lies in the fact that your car can be thrown into the on-coming traffic.

Sometimes, however, in avoiding a head-on crash the choice may be less serious, e.g., damage to another vehicle or mounting a pavement.

A friend of mine recently found himself in a situation when the only way to avoid a head-on smash was to mount the pavement. It was dark and snowing and my friend was driving at about 25 m.p.h. on a very wide road. Suddenly he saw the headlights of what appeared to be a lorry coming straight at him at 60 m.p.h. He waited until the last possible moment for the lorry to swing back to its own side, but in vain. The driver was presumably drunk. At the last moment my friend pulled his car on to the pavement so avoiding a head-on smash. To avoid a head-on accident you may have to drive into someone else going your own way, and the only rule is to do as little damage or injury as possible.

A friend was faced with a drunken dangerous driver coming straight for him. *In order to avoid a collision he watched the front wheels* of the approaching erratic driver. At the last moment my friend swung clear and avoided an accident.

Personally, I would be inclined to check in the driving-mirror, pull in to the near-side (giving the appropriate hand signal) . . . and stop. Obviously, road and traffic conditions at the time determine your actions, but, to weave and dodge about the road could involve other drivers and create confusion or a pile-up.

Centre islands are a common cause of dreadful accidents. A driver tries to overtake, but discovers too late, that he has not left room to get back and hits the bollard. They are specially dangerous in fog or snow.

If you are taking evasive action to avoid an accident, remember that *if it is clear the whole of the road is yours*. Safety of life and limb comes first, even if you have to cross to the wrong side of the road and knock down a hedge.

If driving at a high speed (which I am not recommending), probably somewhere near the middle of the road is safer than too near your own side as this gives you every chance to manoeuvre if anyone steps off the pavement or comes out of a side road. Speed is more dangerous downhill. It takes longer to stop.

Country lanes or quiet roads are DANGEROUS particularly if there are hedges or high banks. FROM A HIDDEN PATH OR GATE A CHILD OR CYCLIST MAY SHOOT OUT. In such places judicious use of the horn can prove to be a life-safer.

In night driving, your headlights, correctly used, help in the matter of safety. They are normally unnecessary in lighted areas where it is courteous to drive with side lights only. Sometimes however, streets are so badly lit that it is necessary for one or both headlights to be used. Do not worry about the other driver, if his eyes are too weak to stand the glare of your lights, this is not your fault. By law your lights cannot exceed a certain strength. If he cannot see, his duty is to slow down or stop ... until he can. It is not your duty to drive "blind" because of him. While driving in the open road, it is courteous to approaching traffic, if safe, to dip your lights but if an approaching motorist puts out both his headlights in the hope of persuading you to do likewise, do not be a fool. Do not drive in the dark.

We speak of glare from headlights, but this is not quite true. Dazzle is largely the result of a reflection on your windscreen. Dazzle is *increased* if you allow your eyes to dwell on the head-lights of the on-coming vehicle. It helps to keep your eyes "off" the approaching lamps. Leaning forward often helps. If your windscreen is one of those that open and you do not mind the draught, you will then find there is practically no dazzle.

The exception might be on a wet road when the reflection from the road causes glare. For those who have fixed windscreens, or do not like so much wind, and have a lot of night driving, it might be worth having a small window cut into the windscreen which could be used when confronted with dazzle. In bad fog opening the windscreen greatly helps vision.

Sometimes, the trouble at night is due to dirty windows. Keep your own windows clear and for wet weather make sure your wipers are in good order.

Courtesy, especially in the dark, should be the order of the considerate motorist. It is frequently possible as well as kind, when following another car, to switch off or at least dip your headlights the reflection of which may be hindering his progress.

When nervous or learner-drivers desire to cross, turn left or right at cross-roads, they are often at a loss to decide which is the moment to proceed.

Think fast! Tell yourself you are not in a car. You want to WALK over the same route that would be driven over. *Walk* not *Run*. If you can walk the same route SAFELY you can DRIVE it. If you would not risk the walk ... do not drive it ... wait.

THE 40 M.P.H. SPEED LIMIT

The 40 m.p.h. speed limit is now in force in various areas. Where in force, there is a prohibited parking zone of 75 ft. from a Pedestrian Crossing as against the 45 ft. on other roads.

Copies of the new speed limit regulations, entitled the "London Traffic (40 m.p.h. Speed Limit) (No. 1) Regulations, 1958," can be obtained from H.M. Stationery Office, London. (Price 4d. Net).

THE ART OF DRIVING

The skilful motorist so positions his car in relation to other traffic and in anticipation of the movement of others, that he rarely, if ever, finds himself in trouble. THIS, PERHAPS ABOVE ALL, IS THE ESSENCE OF ACCIDENT-FREE DRIVING.

CHAPTER THIRTY-FOUR

Life-Savers

TWILIGHT DANGER

Put on side-lights EARLY in the twilight. (Using the battery *helps* it if travelling at 20 m.p.h. or more). Only suicide types delay doing so and our roads are full of them! You do this so that others can see YOU.

SLEEPY DRIVERS

If over-tired stop driving. If you must be a fool and continue (and if you have an accident you may be in trouble in the courts for driving while tired) here are some hints.

> *Singing or whistling helps to keep you awake.*
> *Take off your shoes and drive in stocking feet.*
> *Open a window and allow air to reach your face.*

But, best of all, and all wise long-distance and professional drivers use this method. Draw into a "Lay-by" or side-road and get out. Run or walk about briskly for five to thirty minutes. This not only helps to remove tiredness but to get the eyes focusing correctly again. Eat a bar of chocolate or have some tea. *Don't drink alcohol.*

FOG WARNING

Especially in fog or on wet nights be watchful at traffic lights, particularly in towns as *many* fail to notice them. Keep wind-screen wipers and dipped headlights on.

NIGHT TRAVEL TIP

If driver behind does not dip lights the glare in *your* mirror may be disconcerting. Alter mirror position so that glare is *not* reflected. Reduce speed until overtaken then re-adjust mirror.

DIP HEADLIGHTS

Dip headlights when following close behind another car; do NOT drive on side-lights alone in the dark.

UNDER SNOW

Remember snow-covered cars (especially parked) are less easily seen. Heavy snow is as dangerous as fog. Headlights are a safety help, but if really bad, stop in a safe place.

DRIVER'S WARNING

Remember especially from 6 p.m. onwards many drivers have been celebrating. *Give them lots of room.* Better "The Right Way" than your widow saying in court "He had the right of way".

FOG CAUSES MANY DRIVERS TO BECOME TEMPORARILY INSANE. Half of them drive *so fast* they could not stop if an accident occurred in front. (You can read about them in the Press.) Heavy fog is extremely dangerous, therefore in daylight put on dipped headlights. (It costs nothing). Sidelights are *useless*. Much of the difficulty in fog is due to your front window, in very bad conditions, if you don't have to abandon your car, it helps to put your head out of the window – of course only the experienced driver should do this. The reason for the headlights, is to be *seen, not* to see. At night, in lighted streets, it may be better with side-lights only, also when following other cars.

WET BRAKES

Water can get into brake-linings, so test your brakes after going through floods, heavy rain, or a ford. Make sure when testing that the road is empty and test at low speed, as, if the brakes have been affected, the car may swerve. It is a practical "tip" to press the "foot-pedal" up and down ... hard down ... for 5 minutes or so while the car is stationary. This helps the "drying-out" of the brake-linings. If you have the time it would also help to rest the car for an hour. In any event, have the brakes tested and attended to if necessary.

CARELESS OPENING OF DOORS

The careless opening of doors so as to endanger other road users may be made an offence under the Road Traffic Acts with a much increased maximum penalty of a £50 fine. (R.T.A. 1962.)

CHAPTER THIRTY-FIVE

The Skid and its Correction
(KINETIC ENERGY AND CENTRIFUGAL FORCE)

THE motorist, quite rightly, has a dread that his car may at some time develop a skid. A skid can be disconcerting, and dangerous ... not only to the occupants of the car, but to other motorists, pedestrians and property.

Some skids are of a mild nature and others most serious. The difference between them is of degree only.

You can be positive about one thing, when you skid, *the greater the speed the more vicious and dangerous the result.* Therefore, take heed, look out for the danger signs and danger spots, and, when recognized, prepare to counteract the possible danger immediately ... or it may be too late. It is often wise to stop and test for ice with your foot. Black ice is usually almost invisible apart from testing by foot, but you can sometimes know it exists by an almost imperceptible "weaving" of the car (at rear) or, especially on starting from stop, any wheel-spin.

The first thing is to reduce speed.

For the motor-car there are different kinds of skids. You may be travelling slowly, say ten miles per hours, and you take a fairly sharp turn but the road is slippery. Instantly, you feel your road-wheels slipping. You are apt to become alarmed, especially if there is another vehicle just around the corner, or coming towards you, but because you are travelling slowly you manage to steer clear of trouble.

Visualize yourself in the same situation at 30 to 50 m.p.h. The skid just mentioned was a slight one. Actually, not a skid (in the true sense of the word), but "wheel-spin".

Now, "wheel-spin" is caused by *too* much acceleration on a *greasy* road, particularly on a bend, and this "wheel-spin" reduces the grip exerted by the tyres on the road and allows centrifugal force to act more readily on the car.

"Cement" type of "White" lines can also cause skidding in

inclement weather and should be crossed, when necessary, at an angle.

Incorrect use of brakes and steering can induce a skid. Steering is not improved by braking on a corner. To brake while turning may induce a four-wheel skid. This is the *worst kind of skid* and can cause the car to slide bodily or face the other way.

It is not generally appreciated that in the motivation of a vehicle two distinct dynamic forces become operative:

> A. Centrifugal force.
> B. Kinetic energy.

Draw an imaginary line through the car from the centre of the bonnet the entire length, to the rear. This is the grip exerted on the road by the tyres and propelling the car in a given direction, if you are accelerating.

To deal first with Centrifugal force:—

Imagine lines drawn through your car from the front off-side wheel to just in front of the rear near-side wheel and from the front near-side wheel to the front of the rear off-side wheel, then another line drawn across the car through the point where the previous lines meet; here is created Centrifugal force.

If the centrifugal force is stronger than the "grip" on the road by the tyres (as mentioned previously, i.e., the line drawn from front of car to rear) a skid will result.

In the event of a rear-wheel skid, the method to correct it is as follows: No acceleration. No braking. The car should be steered in the direction in which the rear end of the car is skidding. For a few seconds only, when the car has straightened out, *gently* accelerate. Too much will give you wheel-spin.

Should you ever be unfortunate and get into a four-wheel skid there is little you can do. If you can keep cool, calm and collected ... obviously you will have to think fast ... give quick application of the brake ... and then release. In the event of the front wheels beginning to turn then the method is as for a back-end skid.

We have dealt with centrifugal force, but what is Kinetic energy?

Over thirty years of motoring has brought me into contact with thousands of fellow motorists, and strange as it may seem, not one in one thousand of them had any inkling of the power of this vital force.

Kinetic energy, then, is the moving force possessed by a vehicle in motion. *A small vehicle of one ton doing 40 m.p.h. strikes the same blow as 18 ten-ton steam-rollers travelling at their fastest.*

This is the force you are handling when you speed up a light car to 40 m.p.h. (60 feet per second). If you are driving a two-ton vehicle at 60 m.p.h. (90 feet per second) its kinetic energy is more than that of 100 ten-ton steam-rollers travelling at their highest speed (3 m.p.h.).

ONE-WAY CARRIAGEWAYS AND STREETS

More of these are appearing. The inexperienced driver is apt to panic because traffic moves faster and with cars sometimes passing on either side; it seems confusing. *Do not panic.* These fast drivers are probably very experienced and unlikely to hit you. *Keep calm and go in as straight a line as possible.* You are probably safer here than anywhere.

If you have to leave your "lane" so as to turn off to right (or left) THE SECRETS ARE:

(a) Use your indicator to warn others.
(b) Begin to *very gradually* move towards the final position you require, much *earlier* than you would normally — watch for gaps in the traffic.
(c) Last, but most important, use your mirror and glance over your shoulder. On busy "one-ways" you may have to begin to take up your position as much as half-a-mile before your turning.

NOTE

The author of this book founded THE RIGHT WAY SCHOOLS OF MOTORING. The author resides at 89 Farm Grove Crescent, Cookridge, Leeds, 16, Yorks. (Phone: Leeds 675549). Letters require a stamped self-addressed envelope to ensure a reply.

A FEW OF THE CONTINENTAL TYPE SYMBOLIC SIGNS BEING INTRODUCED IN THE U.K.

END OF MINIMUM
SPEED LIMIT

NO U TURNS

PRIORITY TO VEHICLES
FROM THE OPPOSITE
DIRECTION

SLIPPERY ROAD

GIVE WAY

HORSES OR PONIES

LOW-FLYING AIRCRAFT
OR SUDDEN AIRCRAFT
NOISE

FALLING ROCKS

QUAYSIDE OR RIVER
BANK

DUAL CARRIAGEWAY
ENDS

TWO-WAY TRAFFIC
ACROSS A ONE-WAY
CARRIAGEWAY

STAGGERED JUNCTION

THE HIGHWAY CODE

INCLUDING MOTORWAY RULES

Remember

CHILDREN are in special danger—particularly those under
five and those who cycle. Protect them and train them in road
safety.

OLD PEOPLE may react slowly. Their difficulties are increasing with the continued growth of motor traffic. Give them great
consideration.

THE BLIND also need your help. Give every consideration and
assistance to a person carrying the familiar white walking stick.

HEALTH is important. Be sure you are fit to use the roads.
Make due allowance for poor eyesight, deafness and fatigue in
others.

ALCOHOL, even in quite small amounts, makes you less safe
on the roads. The only safe rule is IF YOU ARE GOING TO DRIVE, DON'T
DRINK. The same applies to drugs even if taken medicinally.

LIGHTS, BRAKES, STEERING and TYRES should be
frequently checked. Lack of maintenance may lead to an accident.

MOTOR CYCLISTS should always wear properly fitting protective helmets.

Issued by the Ministry of Transport

Most road accidents are not "accidents" at all. They need not happen. People die every day on the roads because of carelessness and selfishness.

Casualties — killed and injured — are as high as for a major war. We must not tolerate such a slaughter. We must try to stop it now.

We are building better roads. We want better road users.

This Code tells you just what you must do on the roads to protect lives — your own as well as others.

DO keep to the Code — and keep alive.

Ernest Marples.

Minister of Transport

1961

CONTENTS

THE HIGHWAY CODE

Pedestrians · Dog Owners · Pedal Cyclists · Drivers of Motor Vehicles ·
Motor Cyclists and Riders of Motor-assisted Pedal Cycles · Motorways

PART I

THE ROAD USER ON FOOT

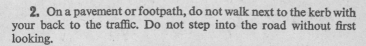

Walking along

1. Where there is a pavement or adequate footpath, use it.

2. On a pavement or footpath, do not walk next to the kerb with your back to the traffic. Do not step into the road without first looking.

3. Where there is no adequate footpath, walk on the right of the road to face oncoming traffic.

4. Do not loiter in the roadway or walk along cycle tracks.

5. A marching body on the road should keep on the left-hand side. It should have look-outs at suitable distances at the front and rear, and at night they should carry lights, white at the front of the column and red at the rear.

Crossing the road

6. Always use subways, footbridges, pedestrian crossings or central refuges when provided. Otherwise cross where you have a clear view of the road both ways. Take extra care if your view is limited by stationary vehicles or other obstructions.

7. Before you cross, STOP AT THE KERB, look right, look left, and right again. Do not cross until the road is clear; then cross at right-angles, keeping a careful look-out all the time.

Where there is a refuge, stop on it in a position where drivers on the far half of the road can easily see you, especially at night. When the road is clear, complete the crossing.

Uncontrolled zebra crossings

8. When you have stepped off the kerb on to a zebra crossing (which must have black and white stripes, studs and lighted beacons), you have the right of way, BUT ALLOW APPROACHING VEHICLES AMPLE TIME TO GIVE WAY, especially if the road is wet or icy.

Do not stand on the pavement at a zebra crossing if you do not intend to cross.

9. Although you have the right of way once you are on the crossing, keep a look-out to right and left as you cross, because a driver's view of you may have been obstructed.

10. Where a zebra crossing has a central refuge, each half is a separate crossing: treat it as such.

Crossing the road at junctions

11. When crossing the road at junctions, look out for vehicles turning the corner.

Signal-controlled crossings

12. At junctions controlled by traffic lights watch the traffic as well as the lights, and cross only when it is safe to do so.

13. If traffic lights have a "CROSS NOW" signal, do not cross until that signal appears.

Police-controlled crossings

14. Do not cross the road, either at a zebra crossing or elsewhere, against a signal to stop by a police officer controlling traffic.

Getting on or off public vehicles

15. Do not get on or off a bus or tram while it is moving, or when it is not at a recognised stopping place. Do not step out suddenly from behind a stationary or slowly moving bus or tram. If you want to get on one at a request stop, give a clear signal for it to stop, and do not step into the road until it has stopped.

PART 2

THE ROAD USER
ON WHEELS

This Part includes rules applicable in general terms to cyclists and those in charge of horses.

Moving off

16. Before you move off, look round, even though you may have looked in your mirror, to see that no one is about to overtake you. Give the proper signal before moving out, and only move off when you can do so safely and without inconvenience to other road users. Give way to passing and overtaking vehicles.

Driving along

17. KEEP WELL TO THE LEFT, except when you intend to overtake or turn right. Do not hug the middle of the road.

18. Do not exceed the speed limits.

Rule 20

19. Never drive at such a speed that you cannot pull up well within the distance you can see to be clear, particularly having regard to the weather and the state of the road.

20. Where there is a double white line along the middle of the road, note whether the one nearer to you is continuous or broken and observe these rules:

—If the line nearer to you is continuous, keep to your own side of it and do not cross or straddle it.

—If the line nearer to you is broken, you may cross it, but only do so if you can complete your overtaking safely and before reaching a continuous white line on your side. A broken line does NOT mean that it is safe for you to overtake.

21. Never cross a single continuous or broken white line along the middle of the road unless you can see that the road well ahead is clear.

22. When following a vehicle on the open road, leave enough space in front of you for an overtaking vehicle.

The safety of pedestrians

23. When approaching ZEBRA CROSSINGS always be ready to slow down or stop so as to give way to pedestrians; *they have the right of way on these crossings.* Signal to other drivers your intention to slow down or stop. Allow yourself more time to stop when the road is wet or icy.

DO NOT OVERTAKE when approaching a ZEBRA CROSSING.

24. At pedestrian crossings controlled by light signals or by the police, give way to pedestrians who are crossing when the signal to move is given.

25. Watch for the pedestrian who comes out suddenly from behind stationary vehicles and other obstructions. Be specially careful of this near schools and bus and tram stops.

26. When turning at a road junction, give way to pedestrians who are crossing.

27. On country roads watch out for pedestrians and give them plenty of room, especially on left-hand bends.

Rule 27

Lane discipline

28. Keep within lane markings and cross them only when moving into another lane. Do not switch from lane to lane. If you wish to move into another lane, do so only when you have given a signal and will not cause inconvenience or danger to other vehicles in it.

29. In traffic hold-ups do not "jump the queue".

30. Well before you reach a junction, make sure you are in the appropriate lane.

Mirror and signals

31. Keep a watch on the traffic behind you by glancing in your mirror. Well before you change direction, overtake or stop, make sure it is safe to do so; look in your mirror (if you are a pedal cyclist or a motor cyclist glance behind) and give a clear signal to indicate your intention.

32. Make sure that your direction indicator gives the signal intended, and that it is cancelled immediately after use.

Overtaking

33. Never overtake unless you KNOW that you can do so without danger to yourself or others. Be specially careful at dusk and in fog or mist, when it is more difficult to judge speed and distance.

34. OVERTAKE ON THE RIGHT.
This rule does not necessarily apply in the following circumstances:

(i) When the driver in front has signalled his intention to turn right and you can overtake him on his left without inconveniencing other traffic, or when you are filtering to the left at a junction.

(ii) In slow-moving congested traffic when vehicles in the lane on your right are moving more slowly than you are.

35. Return to the appropriate lane on the road as soon as practicable after overtaking, but do not cut in sharply in front of the vehicle you have just overtaken.

36. DO NOT OVERTAKE at or when approaching

- —a pedestrian crossing
- —a road junction
- —a corner or bend
- —the brow of a hill
- —a hump-back bridge.

DO NOT OVERTAKE

- —where the road narrows
- —where the road is marked with double white lines and the line nearer to you is continuous if this would involve crossing the continuous line
- —when to do so would force another vehicle to swerve or reduce speed.

IF IN DOUBT – HOLD BACK

Rule 36

Road junctions

37. When approaching a junction with a major road, slow down gradually and if in doubt give way to traffic on the major road. Where there is a "Halt" sign, halt at the major road.

38. At a junction look right, then left, then right again. Do not go on until you are sure that it is safe to do so. Do not rely on signals to go ahead given by unauthorised persons.

39. Well before you turn right at a junction, take full account of the position and movement of following traffic. When safe to do so, signal your intention and take up a position just left of the middle of the road. Wait until there is a safe gap between you and any approaching vehicles before you complete your turn.

40. If you intend to turn left, keep over to the left, signal in good time, and do not swing out to the right either before or after making the turn.

Rule 39

41. At police-controlled junctions let the police officer controlling traffic know clearly by your signal which way you want to go. Do not filter left when straight ahead traffic is held up unless you receive a signal to do so.

42. Where there is a green arrow filter signal at junctions controlled by traffic lights, do not enter the filter lane unless you intend to go in the direction shown by the arrow.

43. Do not go forward when the light is green if it is clear that by doing so you will block the junction when the signals change.

44. When crossing a dual carriageway, treat each carriageway separately, and if necessary wait at the central reservation.

Roundabouts

45. There are no rights of way in general at roundabouts.

Rule 46

Reversing

46. Before you reverse make sure that there are no children or other pedestrians or obstructions in the blind area behind you.

47. Do not reverse from a side road into a main road.

48. If your view to the rear is restricted get help when reversing.

Lights

49. At night always drive well within the limit of your lights.

50. Use dipped headlights at night in built-up areas, unless the street lighting is good.

51.   On unlighted roads always use your headlights. When meeting other vehicles and cyclists dip your headlights. If you are dazzled, slow down or stop.

52.   When driving behind another vehicle dip your headlights.

53.   IN DAYTIME whenever visibility is poor switch on your lights, use headlights in mist or fog to enable other road users to see you more easily.

Stopping and Parking

54.   Do not park or let your vehicle stand

(a) at or near a road junction, a bend, the brow of a hill or a hump-back bridge;

(b) on a footpath;

(c) near traffic lights or a pedestrian crossing;

(d) in a main road or one carrying fast-moving traffic;

(e) opposite or nearly opposite another standing vehicle, a refuge, or other obstruction (e.g. road repairs);

(f) alongside a standing vehicle;

(g) where there is a continuous white line, whether it is accompanied by a broken line or not;

(h) at or near a bus stop, school or hospital entrance, or where it will obscure a traffic sign;

(i) on the "wrong" side of the road at night.

55.   Before opening any door of a vehicle make sure that it will not endanger or inconvenience anybody on the road or footpath. Get out on the kerbside whenever possible.

56.   When you draw up, pull in as close as possible to the edge of the road.

Railway level crossings

57.   At railway level crossing without gates slow down, look both ways, listen and make sure it is safe before crossing the lines. At crossings with gates but no gatekeeper, open *both* gates before starting to cross and do not stop your vehicle on the lines. Close the gates after you.

58. Some level crossings are being equipped with the Continental type of short barrier, which covers only half the width of the road and is worked automatically by approaching trains. The barriers are timed to fall *just before a train reaches the crossing*. Red flashing signals and gongs will be provided, and they will operate before the barriers begin to fall, in order to warn traffic. Do not pass the signals when they are flashing, and do not zigzag round the barriers.

Never cross before the barriers are lifted; there may be a second train coming.

BE PATIENT – NEVER ZIGZAG

Rule 60

EXTRA RULES
FOR PEDAL
CYCLISTS ONLY

59. If there is an adequate cycle track, use it.

60. Ride in single file when road or traffic conditions require it, and never more than two abreast.

61. Never carry anything that may interfere with the proper control of your machine.

62. Do not hold on to another vehicle or another cyclist.

63. Do not ride close behind a moving vehicle.

PART 3

THE ROAD USER
AND ANIMALS

64. Go slowly when driving past animals, and give them plenty of room. Stop if necessary or if signalled to do so. Be prepared to meet led animals coming towards you on your side of the road, especially on a left-hand bend.

65. Do not let your dog stray. When you take it for a walk, or when it is in your car, keep it under close control.

66. Make sure that the road is clear before you let or take animals on to the road.

67. If you are riding a horse, keep to the left.

68. When leading an animal in the road, always place yourself between it and the traffic, and keep the animal to the edge of the road.

69. If you are herding animals along the road and there is someone with you, send him on ahead to warn traffic at danger points such as bends and brows of hills. Carry lights after sunset.

PART 4

MOTORWAY DRIVING

Motorways have no sharp bends, cross-roads, roundabouts or traffic lights. Drivers joining or leaving them always do so from the left. Crossing traffic or right-turning vehicles are carried either above or below. Because of this it is possible to maintain higher average speeds than on other roads.

Safety on motorways is of first importance and it is essential that all who use them should observe strictly the following additional rules.

GENERAL

70. Pedestrians, learner drivers, pedal cycles, motor cycles not exceeding 50 c.c. capacity, invalid carriages, certain vehicles carrying slow-moving oversized loads (except by special permission), agricultural vehicles and animals must not use motorways.

71. Make sure your vehicle is in good condition.

Driving for long spells at an even speed may cause drowsiness. To prevent this, drive with adequate ventilation and stretch your legs at the parking or service areas.

JOINING THE MOTORWAY

72. Look out for the direction signs at the approaches to a motorway so as to avoid joining the wrong carriageway.

73. When joining a motorway at an intermediate access point, you will approach it from the slip road on the left. Watch for a safe gap between vehicles in the nearside traffic lane on the motorway,

and increase your speed in the acceleration lane to the speed of traffic in the nearside lane before joining it.

Give way to traffic already on the motorway.

74. If you discover from route confirmation signs beyond the entrance to a motorway that you are going the wrong way continue until you reach the next exit.

DO NOT REVERSE OR TURN IN THE CARRIAGEWAY OR CROSS THE CENTRAL RESERVATION.

ON THE MOTORWAY

75. Drive at a steady cruising speed comfortably within your capacity and that of your vehicle.

Lane discipline

76. After entering the left-hand traffic lane of a motorway, stay in it long enough to accustom yourself to the speed of vehicles in that lane before attempting to move out into a faster right-hand lane to overtake.

77. KEEP WITHIN THE CARRIAGEWAY LANE MARKINGS and cross them only when changing from one lane to another. Before changing lanes be sure that it is safe to do so, particularly at high speeds. DO NOT WANDER FROM LANE TO LANE.

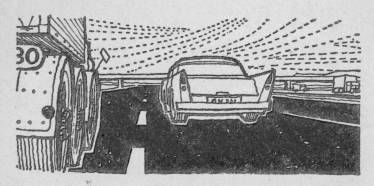

78. On a two-lane carriageway, keep to the left-hand lane except when overtaking.

79. On a three-lane carriageway, you may keep to the centre lane when the left-hand lane is occupied by slower moving vehicles. The outer (right-hand) lane is for overtaking only; do not stay in it longer than is necessary after overtaking vehicles in the centre lane.

80. DO NOT DRIVE TOO CLOSE TO THE VEHICLE AHEAD OF YOU IN YOUR LANE, allow ample distance between your vehicle and the one ahead according to your speed.

Overtaking

81. OVERTAKE ONLY ON THE RIGHT. Right-hand lanes will be free from slow-moving and right-turning vehicles. NEVER OVERTAKE ON THE LEFT.

82. Before pulling out to your right into a traffic lane carrying faster moving traffic, watch out for and GIVE WAY TO TRAFFIC IN LANES TO YOUR RIGHT. USE YOUR MIRROR to make sure that the lane you will be joining is clear for a long distance behind, and bear in mind that an overtaking vehicle may be travelling much faster than you are. Give a clear signal of your intention WELL BEFORE YOU change from one lane to another.

Stopping and parking

83. Do not stop on the carriageway of a motorway except when this is unavoidable or to prevent an accident, or unless required to do so by the police or by an emergency traffic sign.

84. In the event of an emergency or breakdown, pull off the carriageway on to the verge ON THE LEFT, but only for so long as may be necessary (an 8 ft. width of the verge adjacent to the carriageway is constructed as a "hard shoulder" strong enough to carry vehicles leaving the carriageway in an emergency). Before you stop, give a left-turn signal as you decelerate and drive completely on to the verge.

85. Do not park or let your vehicle stand on:

(a) the carriageway;

(b) the slip roads;

(c) the central reservation;

(d) the verges adjacent to the carriageway or slip roads (except in an emergency).

Use instead the parking or service areas with appropriate facilities which are provided at intervals along the motorway.

86. Do not walk on to the carriageways or cross them on foot. Take special care to keep children off the carriageway when you stop in an emergency or at a service area.

Dogs and animals

87. When you stop, whether on the verge or in a service area, or in the event of an accident, keep any animal in your vehicle under close control either in or on a vehicle or held on a lead.

Accidents

88. If you see a knot of vehicles in the distance, which may mean that there has been an accident, reduce speed at once and be prepared to stop.

LEAVING THE MOTORWAY

89. If you are not travelling to the end of the motorway, watch for advance signs warning you of your point of exit.

90. To leave a motorway at one of the intermediate exit points, get into the left-hand lane in good time, stay in it, and give a left-turn signal well before you reach the slip road.

91. Reduce speed as necessary in the deceleration lane on the approach to the slip road.

92. To reach a destination to the right of the motorway, you will leave by a slip road on your left. After leaving the motorway watch for signs directing you to the right via an underpass or a bridge.

93. If you miss your exit, continue along the carriageway until the next exit.

94. When you leave the motorway, remember to adjust your driving to the different conditions of the ordinary road system.

SIGNS AND SIGNALS

DRIVERS AND RIDERS SIGNALS TO OTHER ROAD USERS

These signals should be given by drivers, motor cyclists, pedal cyclists and those in charge of horses. Signal clearly, decisively and in good time. Fully extend the arm. After signalling carry out your intended manoeuvre only when it is safe to do so.

"I intend to MOVE OUT or TURN to my RIGHT"

"I intend to PULL IN or TURN to my LEFT"

"I intend to SLOW DOWN or STOP"

This signal should be used also when slowing down or stopping at a zebra crossing.

DRIVERS AND RIDERS SIGNALS TO POLICE OFFICERS CONTROLLING TRAFFIC

"I want to go STRAIGHT ON"

"I want to TURN LEFT"

"I want to TURN RIGHT"

The left turn and right turn signals may also be given by a mechanical or flashing indicator.

POLICE SIGNALS

Stop

Come On

Vehicle approaching from front

Beckoning on a vehicle from front

Vehicle approaching from behind

Beckoning on a vehicle from behind

Vehicles approaching from both front and behind

Beckoning on a vehicle from the side

TRAFFIC SIGNS

EXAMPLES OF SIGNS WHICH MUST BE OBSERVED

APPROACHES TO MAJOR ROADS

HALT AT MAJOR ROAD AHEAD

Halt until it is safe to go on

SLOW MAJOR ROAD AHEAD

STOP SIGNS

Stop for as long as the sign is displayed

STOP

As used at Road Works

STOP CHILDREN CROSSING

PROHIBITION OR RESTRICTION ON THE USE OF ROADS

SPEED LIMIT **20** M.P.H.

30

40 M.P.H.

Speed Limit Begins

NO RIGHT TURN

NO ENTRY

WAITING LIMITED TO 20 MINS IN ANY HOUR

Posts for signs prohibiting or restricting waiting are normally striped with black and yellow bands

NO WAITING

WEIGHT LIMIT **10** TONS

EXAMPLES OF SIGNS WHICH WARN AND INFORM

| CROSS ROADS | ROAD NARROWS | BEND | ROUND-ABOUT | CROSSING NO GATES | SCHOOL |

SAFETY POSTS & DISCS

Nearside edge of road—red reflectors. Offside—white

Speed Limit Ends

Official Car Park

ADVANCE DIRECTION SIGN

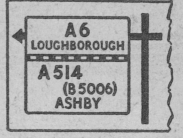

A6 LOUGHBOROUGH

A514 (B5006) ASHBY

A route number in brackets, or a chequer symbol and panel below, indicates a route which may be joined a short distance away in the direction shown.

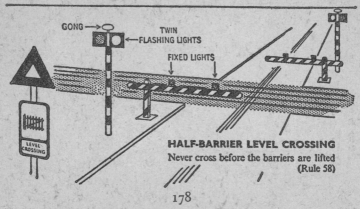

GONG →

TWIN ← FLASHING LIGHTS

FIXED LIGHTS

LEVEL CROSSING

HALF-BARRIER LEVEL CROSSING
Never cross before the barriers are lifted
(Rule 58)

TRAFFIC LIGHT SIGNALS

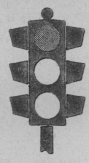  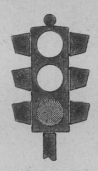

RED means STOP. Wait behind the stop line on the carriageway.

RED and AMBER also means STOP. Do not pass through or start until **GREEN** shows.

GREEN means you may GO ON if the way is clear. Take special care if you mean to turn left or right and give way to pedestrians who are crossing.

AMBER means STOP at the stop line. You may only go on if the **AMBER** appears after you have crossed the stop line or are so close to it that to pull up might cause an accident.

GREEN ARROW means that you may *go in the direction shown by the arrow.* You may do this whatever other lights may be showing.

NOTE: *The signs in this Appendix are not all drawn to the same scale.*

THE LAW'S DEMANDS

Revised 1963

The following pages deal with major points of the law affecting safety on the roads. For the precise wording of the law you should refer to the various Acts and Regulations. These are indicated in the margin by the following abbreviations:

B.P.C.R. Brakes on Pedal Cycle Regulations, 1954.

C.U.R. Motor Vehicles (Construction and Use) Regulations, 1955.

D.L.R. Motor Vehicles (Driving Licences) Regulations, 1950.

H.A. Highway Act, 1835, or, as the case may be, Highways Act, 1959.

L.A. Licensing Act, 1872.

M.R. Motorways Traffic Regulations, 1959.

P.C.(P.B.C.)R. Pedestrian Crossings (Push Button Control) Regulations, 1962.

P.C.R. Pedestrian Crossings Regulations, 1954.

R.T.A. Road Traffic Acts, 1960 and 1962.

R.T.L.A. Road Transport Lighting Acts, 1957 and 1958.

R.V.L.R. Road Vehicles Lighting Regulations, 1959.

R.V.L. (Ex.) R. Road Vehicles Lighting (Standing Vehicles) (Exemption) Regulations, 1955 and 1956.

S.L.S.R. Motor Vehicles (Speed Limits on Special Roads) Regulations, 1959.

T.R. Motor Vehicles (Tests) Regulations, 1960.

V.E.A. Vehicles (Excise) Act, 1962.

TO PEDESTRIANS

P.C.R. No. 4
P.C.(P.B.C.)R.
No. 7

You have precedence when you are on the carriageway within limits of an uncontrolled zebra crossing, and of a push button controlled panda crossing during the period when the word "CROSS" in the signals is illuminated.

NOTES: (a) An uncontrolled zebra crossing is one at which traffic is not being controlled by a police officer and which is marked with two or more lighted beacons, black and white stripes, and studs indicate the limits of the crossing.
(b) You have NO precedence when you are standing on the kerb or when you are standing on a street refuge or central reservation which is on a zebra crossing, or at a push button controlled panda crossing when no lights are showing or when the word "WAIT" is illuminated.

YOU MUST NOT

P.C.R. No. 8
P.C.(P.B.C.)R.
No. 11

loiter on any type of pedestrian crossing;

H.A. 1959
Sect. 121

wilfully obstruct the free passage along a highway;

R.T.A. 1960
Sect. 15

proceed along or across the carriageway when given a direction to stop by a police officer in uniform engaged in controlling traffic;

R.T.A. 1960
Sects. 218 & 219

without lawful authority or reasonable cause, hold on to or get on a motor vehicle or trailer in motion or tamper with the brake or other part of the mechanism of a motor vehicle;

L.A. Sect. 12

be drunk in any highway or public place.

TO DOG OWNERS

YOU MUST NOT

R.T.A. 1960
Sect. 220

allow your dog to be off its lead on a road which has been designated as one where dogs must be kept on a lead, unless your dog is kept for tending sheep or cattle or is in use under proper control for sporting purposes.

TO PEDAL CYCLISTS

Before cycling, MAKE SURE THAT

B.P.C.R. Nos. 3-5

your cycle has efficient brakes. (A bicycle must have an independent brake on each wheel except that if no wheel exceeds 18″ in diameter including tyre, only one brake is needed, and a fixed-wheel bicycle need have only one brake but that brake must operate on the front wheel. For tricycles see the Regulations.)

YOU MUST, even if you are wheeling your cycle,

R.T.A. 1960 Sect. 14	observe traffic signs and signals and the directions of a police officer controlling traffic;
R.T.A. 1960 Sect. 48	stop when signalled to do so by a School Crossing Patrol;
P.C.R. No. 4	give precedence to pedestrians on an uncontrolled zebra crossing, that is, a crossing marked by black and white stripes, studs and lighted beacons and at which there is no police officer controlling the traffic.
P.C. (P.B.C.) R. No. 7	give precedence to pedestrians on a push button controlled panda crossing during the period when the flashing amber light is showing.

NOTE: The pulsating amber and red lights in these crossings have the same meaning as similarly coloured steady lights when shown alone in light signals (See page 179).

YOU MUST

R.T.L.A. 1957 Sects. 1, 6 & 17	at night, see that your front and rear lamps are alight and that your cycle has an efficient red reflector;
R.T.L.A. 1957 Sect. 6	at night, if you are wheeling your cycle or are stationary without lights, keep as close as possible to the nearside edge of the road;
R.T.A. 1960 Sect. 223	stop when required to do so by a police officer in uniform.

YOU MUST NOT

P.C.R. No. 5 P.C. (P.B.C.) R. No. 8	stop your cycle within the limits of any type of pedestrian crossing, except in circumstances beyond your control or when it is necessary to do so to avoid an accident;
R.T.A. 1960 Sect. 9	ride recklessly or at a speed or in a manner which is dangerous to the public;
„ 10	ride without due care and attention or without reasonable consideration for other persons using the road;
„ 11	ride under the influence of drink or a drug;
H.A. 1835 Sect. 72	wilfully ride on a footpath by the side of any road made or set apart for the use of foot-passengers;
H.A. 1835 Sect. 78	by negligence or misbehaviour interrupt the free passage of any road user or vehicle;
R.T.A. 1960 Sect. 16	leave your cycle on any road in such a way that it is likely to cause danger to other road users;
R.T.A. 1960 Sects. 26 & 34 R.T.A. 1962 Sect. 28	leave your cycle where waiting is prohibited;
R.T.A. 1960 Sect. 13	carry a passenger on a bicycle not constructed or adapted to carry more than one person;
R.T.A. 1960 Sect. 219	hold on to a motor vehicle or trailer in motion on any road.

TO DRIVERS OF MOTOR VEHICLES
Before driving, MAKE SURE THAT

V.E.A. Sect. 1	your vehicle is properly licensed;
R.T.A. 1960 Sect. 201	your insurance is in order, i.e. that it covers the liabilities in respect of third party risks of yourself and any other person who may use your vehicle;
R.T.A. 1960 Sect. 98 and D.L.R. No. 17	you have a driving licence valid for the class of vehicle which you intend to drive, that it is not out of date, and that you have signed it in ink;
T.R.	you have a current test certificate for your vehicle if it is over the prescribed age limit;
R.T.A. 1962 Sect. 42	your eyesight is up to the standard required for the driving test;
R.T.A. 1960 Sect. 6(1) R.T.A. 1962 Sect. 1	you are not under the influence of drink or a drug;
C.U.R. No. 73(1)	the condition of your vehicle and of any trailer it may be drawing and of all parts and accessories is such that no danger is likely to be caused to yourself or others;
C.U.R. No. 76 (1) & (2)	your brakes and steering are in good working order and properly adjusted;
C.U.R. No. 78	your tyres are free from defects likely to cause damage to the road or danger to yourself or others;
C.U.R. Nos. 75 & 76(3)	your windscreen is clean and the windscreen wiper in working order;
C.U.R. No. 16	your vehicle has a mirror (two if it is not a private car) so fitted that you can see traffic behind you;
C.U.R. No. 19	your horn is in working order;
C.U.R. No. 74	your speedometer is in working order;
C.U.R. No. 77(2)	your silencer is efficient;
C.U.R. No. 73(2)	the load on your vehicle is not excessive or so badly distributed, packed or secured as to be dangerous;
C.U.R. No. 102 and 102A R.T.L.A. 1957 Sect. 1 and R.V.L.R. No. 25	your load if it projects sideways or to the front or rear is not of illegal width or length and at night any extra front and rear lights are carried;
R.T.L.A. 1957 R.V.L.R. and C.U.R. Nos 24A & 76A	your vehicle has lights and reflectors which comply with the regulations and are in working order;
R.V.L.R. Nos. 8 & 9	your headlights comply in particular with the anti-dazzle requirements.

183

When driving YOU MUST

C.U.R. No. 86 be in such a position that you can exercise proper control over your vehicle and retain a full view of the road and traffic ahead;

P.C.R. No. 4 give precedence to a pedestrian who is on an uncontrolled zebra crossing, that is, a crossing marked by black and white stripes, studs and lighted beacons and at which there is no police officer controlling the traffic;

P.C. (P.B.C.) R. No. 7 give precedence to pedestrians on a push button controlled panda crossing during the period when the flashing amber light is showing.

NOTE: The pulsating amber and red lights in these crossings have the same meaning as similarly coloured steady lights when shown alone in light signals (See page 179).

R.T.A. 1960 Sects. 4, 19, 24 and First Schedule R.T.A. 1962 Sections 11 and 13 observe speed limits or any speed limit to which your type of vehicle is subject;

R.T.A. 1960 Sect. 14 observe traffic signs and signals and the direction of a police officer controlling traffic;

R.T.A. 1960 Sect. 223 stop when required to do so by a police officer in uniform;

R.T.A. 1960 Sect. 48 stop when signalled to do so by a School Crossing Patrol;

R.T.L.A. 1957 Sect. 1 see that your side and tail lamps are alight at night.

YOU MUST NOT

R.T.A. 1960 Sect. 2 drive recklessly or at a speed or in a manner which is dangerous to the public;

R.T.A. 1960 Sect. 3 drive without due care and attention or without reasonable consideration for other persons using the road;

R.T.A. 1960 Sect. 6(1) R.T.A. 1962 Sect. 1 drive under the influence of drink or a drug;

C.U.R. No. 79 drive a vehicle which emits excessive fumes and smoke;

C.U.R. No. 81 drive a vehicle which is excessively noisy;

C.U.R. No. 84 sound your horn at night (11.30 p.m.—7 a.m.) in a built-up area.

When you stop YOU MUST

C.U.R. No. 91 stop the engine and set the brake before you leave the vehicle;

R.V.L.R. No. 12 R.T.L.A. 1957 Sect. 1 and R.V.L. (Ex.) R. 1955 & 1956 switch off your headlights at night, but see that your side and tail lamps are alight; on some roads governed by a speed limit, there are certain exemptions from showing side and tail lights when standing or parked in compliance with specified conditions;

R.T.A. 1960 Sects. 225 & 226 when required by the police, produce your driving licence, certificate of insurance and, if your vehicle is subject to compulsory testing, your test certificate, for examination. If necessary, you may instead produce them within 5 days at any police station you select.

YOU MUST NOT

P.C.R. No. 6 P.C. (P.B.C.) R. No. 9	stop your vehicle on the approach side of an uncontrolled zebra crossing or a push button controlled panda crossing beyond the double line of studs in the road (which are usually 15 yards from the crossing where there is a 30 m.p.h. speed limit or 25 yards where there is a higher or no speed limit) except to give precedence to a pedestrian on the crossing, or in circumstances beyond your control, or when it is necessary to do so to avoid an accident;
P.C.R. No. 5 P.C. (P.B.C.) R. No. 8	stop your vehicle within the limits of any type of pedestrian crossing, except in circumstances beyond your control, or to avoid an accident;
C.U.R. No. 89	park your vehicle or trailer on the road so as to cause unnecessary obstruction;
R.T.A. 1960 Sect. 16	park your vehicle or trailer on the road in such a way that it is likely to cause danger to other road users;
C.U.R. No. 90	park at night on the "wrong" side of the road;
R.T.A. 1960 Sects. 26, 34 & 88 R.T.A. 1962 Sect. 28	park your vehicle contrary to waiting restrictions; on a clearway you must not stop your vehicle on the carriageway, and in a parking zone you must not park except at a meter.
C.U.R. No. 84	sound your horn while stationary.

If you are involved in an accident

R.T.A. 1960 Sects. 77 & 226	which causes damage or injury to any other person, or other vehicle, or any animal (horse, cattle, ass, mule, sheep, pig, goat or dog) not in your vehicle;

YOU MUST

(a) stop;

(b) give your own and the vehicle owner's name and address and the registration mark of the vehicle to anyone having reasonable grounds for requiring them;

(c) if you do not give your name and address to any such person at the time, report the accident to the police as soon as reasonably practicable, and in any case within 24 hours;

(c) if anyone is injured and you do not produce your certificate of insurance at the time to the police or to anyone who has with reasonable grounds required its production, report the accident to the police as soon as possible, and in any case within 24 hours, and produce your certificate of insurance to the police, either when reporting the accident or within 5 days thereafter at any police station you select.

TO MOTOR CYCLISTS and RIDERS of MOTOR-ASSISTED PEDAL CYCLES

Most of the requirements of the law relating to motor drivers, including those relating to pedestrian crossings, apply to you. In addition:

YOU MUST NOT

R.T.A. 1960 Sect. 8 and C.U.R. No. 101
carry more than one passenger on a two-wheeled machine, and the passenger must sit astride the cycle on a proper seat securely fitted behind the driver's seat and with proper rests for the feet.

R.T.A. 1960 Sect. 88
park in a parking meter zone except at a meter or in a specially marked motor cycle park.

MOTORWAYS

S.L.S.R.
There is no speed limit except for one of 40 m.p.h. for motor vehicles drawing a trailer (excluding articulated vehicles) if the trailer has less than four wheels or is a close-coupled four-wheeled trailer.

TO DRIVERS OF MOTOR VEHICLES AND MOTOR CYCLISTS ON MOTORWAYS

YOU MUST

M.R. No. 5
drive on the carriageways only;

M.R. No. 6
observe one-way driving on the carriageways;

M.R. No. 13
keep any animals in your charge in the vehicle or under proper control on the verge.

YOU MUST NOT

M.R. No. 11
use the motorway if you are a learner driver;

M.R. No. 8
reverse on the carriageways;

M.R. No. 7(1)
stop on the carriageways;

M.R. No. 9
stop on the verges except in emergency;

M.R. No. 10
stop on the central reservation;

M.R. No. 12
walk on the carriageway or on the central reservation except in emergency.

186

FIRST AID on the road

When an accident happens:

Control traffic so as to avoid further accident (ask motorists and bystanders for help in this).

Move casualty only if there is immediate danger of fire from spilled petrol (no smoking) or if danger from traffic cannot be averted. Where the casualty must be moved, handle with great care, particularly if broken bones are suspected or pain in the back is complained of.

Stop bleeding with dry dressings or clean handkerchiefs and firm manual pressure; bandage firmly with handkerchief or scarf.

Cover burns with dry dressings or clean handkerchiefs and bandage with handkerchief or scarf.

Get help immediately. Get motorists and bystanders to summon ambulance, doctor, police.

Keep casualty lying down and warm. Use rugs or coats below as well as above.

Do not move casualty if it can be avoided until skilled attention is available.

Do not give anything to drink— alcohol, tea or other fluid. (Casualty may require anæsthetic at hospital.)

Be prepared: Carry simple first aid materials in your car, and learn first aid from the St. John Ambulance Association, St. Andrew's Ambulance Association or British Red Cross Society.

When visiting the countryside PLEASE REMEMBER

GUARD AGAINST ALL RISK OF FIRE
FASTEN ALL GATES
KEEP DOGS UNDER PROPER CONTROL
KEEP TO PATHS ACROSS FARM LAND
AVOID DAMAGING FENCES, HEDGES AND WALLS
LEAVE NO LITTER
SAFEGUARD WATER SUPPLIES
PROTECT WILD LIFE, WILD PLANTS, AND TREES
GO CAREFULLY ON COUNTRY ROADS
RESPECT THE LIFE OF THE COUNTRYSIDE

From "THE COUNTRY CODE" booklet, prepared by the National Parks Commission and published by Her Majesty's Stationery Office. Price 4d. net.

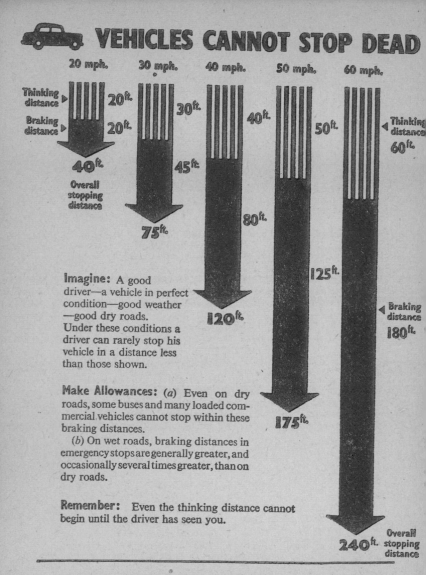

VEHICLES CANNOT STOP DEAD

20 mph. 30 mph. 40 mph. 50 mph. 60 mph.

Thinking distance ▷ 20ft.
Braking distance ▷ 20ft.
40ft. Overall stopping distance

30ft.
45ft.
75ft.

40ft.
80ft.
120ft.

50ft.
125ft.
175ft.

Thinking distance ◁ 60ft.
Braking distance ◁ 180ft.
240ft. Overall stopping distance

Imagine: A good driver—a vehicle in perfect condition—good weather —good dry roads. Under these conditions a driver can rarely stop his vehicle in a distance less than those shown.

Make Allowances: (*a*) Even on dry roads, some buses and many loaded commercial vehicles cannot stop within these braking distances.

(*b*) On wet roads, braking distances in emergency stops are generally greater, and occasionally several times greater, than on dry roads.

Remember: Even the thinking distance cannot begin until the driver has seen you.

PREPARED BY THE MINISTRY OF TRANSPORT AND THE
CENTRAL OFFICE OF INFORMATION

The Highway Code may be purchased direct from *Her Majesty's Stationery Office* at the following addresses: York House, Kingsway, London, W.C.2; 423 Oxford Street, London, W.1; 13a Castle Street, Edinburgh 2; 39 King Street, Manchester 2; 2 Edmund Street, Birmingham 3; 109 St. Mary Street, Cardiff; 50 Fairfax Street, Bristol 1; 80 Chichester Street, Belfast; or through any bookseller.

Printed in England under the authority of Her Majesty's Stationery Office
Reprinted with amendments 1961

INDEX

AN APPEAL

IF YOU HAVE FOUND THIS BOOK USEFUL I WOULD BE
IF YOU WOULD TELL YOUR DRIVING INSTRUCTOR, BO
AND FRIENDS WHAT YOU THINK OF IT. IN THIS WAY WE
BE ABLE TO INCREASE THE SALES TO ENABLE US TO REC
THOUSANDS OF POUNDS A YEAR WE SPEND ON SUCH
PUBLICITY AND ADVERTISING. RESEARCH TO KEEP THE
TO DATE ALSO COSTS MONEY. THE AUTHOR, MR. NATE
DEVOTED HIS LIFE TO DRIVING INSTRUCTION. HE HAS MA
'LABOUR OF LOVE.'
WE MAKE THIS REQUEST IN THE INTEREST OF SAFETY –
YOU.

And
P

Companion volume

CAR REPAIRS PROPERLY EXPLAINED

A new book to give everybody insight into that perplexing
the modern (or ancient) car. Covers: Charging System,
System, Tyres, Suspension, Brakes, Cooling System, Fuel
Lubrication, Electrical Fault Finding, etc. Another WINNER fr

ELLIOT RIGHT WAY BOOKS,
KINGSWOOD BUILDINGS,
KINGSWOOD, SURREY.